The European Framework of Credit Intermediaries

Umberto Filotto • Francesco Ruggiero •
Dario Sgrulletti
Editors

The European Framework of Credit Intermediaries

Entities, Supervisory Authorities, and Regulatory Frameworks in Credit Distribution

Editors
Umberto Filotto
Tor Vergata University of Rome
Rome, Italy

Dario Sgrulletti
Tor Vergata University of Rome
Rome, Italy

Francesco Ruggiero
OAM - Organismo per la gestione degli Elenchi degli Agenti in attività finanziaria e dei Mediatori creditizi
Rome, Italy

ISBN 978-3-032-05941-3   ISBN 978-3-032-05942-0 (eBook)
https://doi.org/10.1007/978-3-032-05942-0

© The Editor(s) (if applicable) and The Author(s) 2026. This book is an open access publication.
Open Access This book is licensed under the terms of the Creative Commons Attribution 4.0 International License (http://creativecommons.org/licenses/by/4.0/), which permits use, sharing, adaptation, distribution and reproduction in any medium or format, as long as you give appropriate credit to the original author(s) and the source, provide a link to the Creative Commons license and indicate if changes were made.
The images or other third party material in this book are included in the book's Creative Commons license, unless indicated otherwise in a credit line to the material. If material is not included in the book's Creative Commons license and your intended use is not permitted by statutory regulation or exceeds the permitted use, you will need to obtain permission directly from the copyright holder.
The use of general descriptive names, registered names, trademarks, service marks, etc. in this publication does not imply, even in the absence of a specific statement, that such names are exempt from the relevant protective laws and regulations and therefore free for general use.
The publisher, the authors and the editors are safe to assume that the advice and information in this book are believed to be true and accurate at the date of publication. Neither the publisher nor the authors or the editors give a warranty, expressed or implied, with respect to the material contained herein or for any errors or omissions that may have been made. The publisher remains neutral with regard to jurisdictional claims in published maps and institutional affiliations.

This Palgrave Macmillan imprint is published by the registered company Springer Nature Switzerland AG.
The registered company address is: Gewerbestrasse 11, 6330 Cham, Switzerland.

If disposing of this product, please recycle the paper.

Produced by the OAM Research Office and the University of Rome 'Tor Vergata'.

Preface

This study explores the framework of credit intermediation and distribution in Europe, providing an overview of the credit distribution sector across the following member states: Belgium, France, Germany, Portugal, Spain and Italy. Additionally, the framework of the United Kingdom is analysed. A credit intermediary in Europe is generally defined as an individual or firm that facilitates access to credit provided by third-party credit providers, typically banks, without directly providing the credit themselves. These intermediaries include financial agents, credit brokers and point-of-sale retailers, serving both consumers and businesses. While the exact definition and regulatory requirements for credit intermediaries can vary between countries, their activity remains consistent in supporting credit access and market operations. Credit intermediaries in Europe are subject to a diverse range of regulatory requirements depending on the specific credit product and national legislation. Generally, there is a hierarchical structure where mortgage credit intermediation is the most stringently regulated, followed by consumer credit. Intermediaries must obtain specific licenses to operate, demonstrating trustworthiness, financial stability and competence in credit products and services. Main licensing criteria include evidence of good reputation, adequate financial resources and appropriate knowledge, structure and competence. Regulatory bodies and authorities, often at the national or regional level, oversee the licensing and compliance of credit intermediaries, ensuring adherence to legal and professional standards. Credit intermediaries across Europe are required to adhere to high standards of professional conduct, acting fairly and in good faith. They must possess adequate knowledge and competence in credit mediation and financial products, and provide objective advice tailored to the customer's profile. Transparency is transversely a foundation of credit intermediation, with intermediaries obligated to disclose their identity, the nature of their services, any affiliations with credit providers and all relevant pre-contractual and contractual information. Disclosure rules mandate that intermediaries inform consumers of any fees, commissions and the specifics of the credit agreements they facilitate. These transparency measures aim to protect consumers and ensure informed decision-making. The supervision of credit intermediaries is typically conducted by financial supervisory authorities at the national or regional level. These authorities ensure that intermediaries comply with licensing requirements and professional standards, contributing to the stability and integrity of the credit market.

Rome, Italy	Umberto Filotto
Rome, Italy	Francesco Ruggiero
Rome, Italy	Dario Sgrulletti

COMPETING INTERESTS

The authors declare no competing financial or non-financial interests in relation to the content of this book. This work is the result of independent academic research conducted jointly by the University of Rome "Tor Vergata" and the *Organismo Agenti in attività finanziaria e dei Mediatori creditizi* (OAM). No commercial or institutional interest has influenced the research process, content, or conclusions.

ACKNOWLEDGEMENTS

The authors wish to express their sincere gratitude to the many institutions and professionals who have provided valuable insights, regulatory documentation and formal responses, which have significantly contributed to the comparative analysis presented in this volume.

In Belgium, we thank the *Union Professionnelle du Crédit* (UPC) and Federation of the Belgian Financial Sector (Febelfin) for their detailed and timely contributions concerning the legal framework governing credit intermediation and the national licensing systems. For France, we are especially grateful to the *Association Française des Sociétés Financières* (ASF) for their input and support in outlining the regulatory environment for credit intermediaries. In Germany, the *Bankenfachverband e.V.* has played a key role by providing a structured overview of the national legal framework, licensing requirements and supervisory landscape, which served as a fundamental reference point for the German chapter. In Portugal, we are thankful to the *Associação de Instituições de Crédito Especializado* (ASFAC), whose contributions and technical clarifications greatly enhanced the understanding of the Portuguese credit intermediation system. The Spanish chapter benefited immensely from the collaboration with the *Asociación Nacional de Establecimientos Financieros de Crédito* (ASNEF), whose institutional response provided valuable insights into Spanish regulatory and market practices. For the United Kingdom, we express our sincere appreciation to the Finance & Leasing Association (FLA), whose comprehensive report on the UK's regulatory framework – particularly with reference to the Financial Conduct Authority (FCA) – greatly enriched the analysis.

Finally, we wish to thank the many compliance officers and legal experts who supported this research through interviews, technical feedback and the sharing of key regulatory documents. This volume would not have been possible without their cooperation, expertise and commitment to clarity and rigour in the study of European credit intermediation.

Ethics Approval

The analysis is based solely on publicly available regulatory texts, official communications from supervisory authorities and legal and institutional frameworks across the countries under examination.

About the Book

This study aims to examine the legal and regulatory frameworks governing the credit distribution sector in the main European countries, including Belgium, France, Germany, Italy, Portugal, Spain and the United Kingdom. The analysis focuses on both the legal structures and the market dynamics within each country, with particular emphasis on the roles of financial agents and credit brokers.

Methodological Note

The data for this study were primarily collected through a standardised questionnaire distributed to relevant regulatory authorities in each country. The questionnaire was designed to gather detailed information on the legal frameworks, oversight mechanisms, industry practices and challenges faced by credit intermediaries. This method ensured the collection of consistent and comparable data across countries.

Questionnaire Structure

The questionnaire consisted of five sections:

- Legal framework: questions on the specific laws governing credit distribution, including transposed EU directives and national legal instruments.
- Regulatory authorities: questions regarding the oversight bodies responsible for supervising credit intermediaries and enforcing compliance with national and EU regulations.
- Industry structure: a set of questions aimed at identifying the main actors in the credit distribution sector, including financial agents, credit brokers and non-bank entities.
- Professional conduct: this section focused on the standards of professional conduct, including voluntary codes of practice and regulatory requirements related to transparency, fairness and consumer protection.
- Challenges and best practices: questions that explored the specific challenges faced by the industry, such as regulatory complexity, the cost of compliance and adapting to technological changes, as well as the best practices employed in each jurisdiction.

Data Processing

Once collected, the responses were standardised and categorised based on predefined themes: regulatory authority, regulatory approach, licensing requirements, voluntary standards and main challenges.

Comparative Analysis

The comparative framework was established by aligning the core themes across all countries. Main differences and similarities in the regulatory approach, licensing requirements and the role of voluntary industry standards were highlighted. The questionnaire data allowed for direct comparison of national frameworks, offering insights into how different countries address common issues, such as consumer protection, risk management and market transparency.

LIMITATIONS

As legal frameworks in Europe continue to evolve, especially with the introduction of new EU directives, this study provides a snapshot of the frameworks as they existed at the time of data collection.

CONCLUSION

The methodology of using a standardised questionnaire enabled the study to present a thorough and uniform analysis of credit distribution across European countries. This approach offers valuable insights into the interplay between national and EU regulations and provides a clear understanding of the industry's regulatory and operational framework across the region.

Contents

1	Introduction	1
2	**Belgium**	13
	Credit Intermediaries in Belgium	14
	Credit Intermediary and Licensing Requirements for Credit Intermediaries	16
	Laws and Relevant Authorities in Belgium	20
3	**France**	23
	Credit Intermediaries in France	24
	Credit Intermediary and Licensing Requirements for Credit Intermediaries	28
	Laws and Relevant Authorities in France	33
4	**Germany**	37
	Credit Intermediaries in Germany	38
	Credit Intermediary and Licensing Requirements for Credit Intermediaries	39
	Laws and Relevant Authorities in Germany	40
5	**Italy**	43
	Credit Intermediaries in Italy	44

		Credit Intermediary and Licensing Requirements for Credit Intermediaries	48
		Laws and Relevant Authorities in Italy	54
6	**Portugal**		57
		Credit Intermediaries in Portugal	58
		Credit Intermediary and Licensing Requirements for Credit Intermediaries	60
		Laws and Relevant Authorities in Portugal	64
7	**Spain**		67
		Credit Intermediaries in Spain	68
		Credit Intermediary and Licensing Requirements for Credit Intermediaries	70
		Laws and Relevant Authorities in Spain	73
8	**United Kingdom**		77
		Credit Intermediaries in the UK	78
		Credit Intermediary and Licensing Requirements for Credit Intermediaries	83
		Laws and Relevant Authorities in the UK	85
9	**Comparative Analysis**		93
10	**Conclusions**		103

CHAPTER 1

Introduction

Abstract This chapter introduces the study of credit intermediation in Europe. It outlines its scope, objectives, and methodological approach. It defines the role of credit intermediaries as facilitators between credit providers and borrowers and introduces the countries analysed (Belgium, France, Germany, Italy, Portugal, Spain, and the United Kingdom). The chapter highlights the economic relevance of credit distribution, the diversity of regulatory frameworks, and the importance of consumer protection and transparency. It also provides an overview of the standardized questionnaire methodology adopted to ensure comparability across jurisdictions.

Keywords credit intermediation • European Union • methodology • regulation • consumer protection • transparency • market access

This chapter introduces the regulatory and operational frameworks on credit intermediaries across key jurisdictions, provides an overview and compares national approaches, highlighting both harmonisation efforts and persistent fragmentation in the sector.

Overview of Credit Intermediation in Europe

The financial framework in Europe is characterised by a diverse and complex system of credit intermediation that facilitates access to credit for both consumers and businesses. Credit intermediaries, defined as entities or individuals that facilitate access to credit without directly providing it, are essential actors in the financial ecosystem. They bridge the gap between credit providers (e.g., banks) and borrowers, ensuring that credit products are accessible, transparent and tailored to end-users' needs. This study examines the regulatory and operational frameworks governing credit intermediaries across six European jurisdictions (Belgium, France, Germany, Italy, Portugal and Spain) and one non-European jurisdiction (the United Kingdom). Each of these countries has developed a specific approach to the regulation of credit intermediation, despite the common goal of achieving a minimum level of harmonisation, reflecting their distinct legal traditions, market structures and consumer protection priorities. In designing this comparative study, particular attention was devoted to ensuring consistency and clarity across all chapters. Each jurisdictional analysis follows a common structure – covering the classification of credit intermediaries, authorisation and registration requirements, applicable legal and regulatory sources and the role of supervisory authorities. This harmonised format was adopted to facilitate cross-country comparison and enhance the readability of the volume. As for the selection of the countries examined – Italy, France, Germany, Spain, Belgium, Portugal and the United Kingdom – these were chosen based on a combination of relevance, diversity and regulatory significance within the European context. The sample includes both founding EU Member States and countries representing different legal contexts and institutional models. Moreover, the inclusion of the United Kingdom, despite its exit from the European Union, provides additional comparative insight, particularly given ongoing regulatory divergence. The selected jurisdictions also reflect the availability of mature and publicly accessible regulatory frameworks, which contributed to a well-documented analysis.

The European Union has sought to harmonise certain aspects of credit intermediation through directives, including the Mortgage Credit Directive (MCD) and the Consumer Credit Directive (CCD). However, significant differences remain in how Member States implement these regulations, resulting in a still-fragmented regulatory environment. This study provides an overview of these frameworks and highlights both the commonalities and divergences in credit intermediary regulation. This analysis examines, among other aspects, the legal definitions, licensing requirements, legal obligations and supervisory mechanisms, along with the main national authorities in each jurisdiction. The report also highlights the challenges and opportunities facing credit intermediaries in Europe.

Credit intermediaries operate in a variety of forms, including financial agents and credit brokers. Their activities range from facilitating mortgage loans to arranging consumer credit for goods and services. Despite their diversity, all credit intermediaries share the common goal of facilitating access to credit while ensuring compliance with legal and professional standards. This study explores how these intermediaries operate within different regulatory environments and how they balance market efficiency with consumer protection.

The importance of credit intermediaries in the European financial system cannot be underestimated. They are central actors as they promote financial inclusion, and they enable individuals and businesses to access credit. At the same time, they must deal, in certain cases, with a complex web of regulations designed to protect consumers and maintain the integrity of the financial system. This study provides a detailed analysis of these regulatory frameworks, lists the main laws governing the sector and offers insights into the challenges credit intermediaries face and the strategies they employ to meet their obligations.

THE ROLE OF CREDIT INTERMEDIARIES IN FINANCIAL MARKETS

As noted earlier, credit intermediaries are essential to financial markets, serving as conduits between credit providers and borrowers. Their role extends beyond mere facilitation; they provide valuable services such as financial advice, product comparison and tailored recommendations. By doing so, they help borrowers make informed decisions and access credit products that best meet their needs. This section explores the multifaceted role of credit intermediaries in financial markets, focusing on national-level legal definitions that clarify how financial intermediaries are perceived and regulated in each country.

A relevant function of credit intermediaries is to enhance market efficiency by reducing information asymmetry between borrowers and lenders. Borrowers often lack the knowledge and expertise to completely understand the complex features of credit products, while lenders may struggle to assess the creditworthiness of potential borrowers or to reach specific markets to enrich their distribution models. Credit intermediaries bridge this gap through expert advice and transaction facilitation. They help borrowers understand credit agreement terms, compare products and select the most suitable options. At the same time, they assist lenders in identifying creditworthy borrowers and managing risk, and deliver products in a professional manner to markets that could not be otherwise served by the lenders.

Beyond promoting market efficiency, credit intermediaries contribute to consumer protection. They are subject to stringent regulatory requirements designed to ensure that they act in the best interests of their clients. These requirements include obligations to provide transparent and accurate information, avoid conflicts of interest and adhere to high standards of professional conduct. Compliance with these regulations helps protect consumers from predatory lending and ensures fair treatment.

Credit intermediaries also contribute to financial stability by promoting responsible lending practices, as they are required to assess the creditworthiness of borrowers and ensure that credit products are suitable for their financial circumstances. This helps prevent over-indebtedness and reduces the risk of default, which can have systemic implications for the financial system. Furthermore, credit intermediaries are often subject to ongoing supervision by regulatory authorities, which helps ensure that they comply with legal and professional standards.

Despite their importance, credit intermediaries face significant challenges in fulfilling their responsibilities. These include acting in a complex regulatory framework, managing conflicts of interest and adapting to technological changes. This study examines these aspects in detail, offering insights into how credit intermediaries can address them and remain active in financial markets.

In many of the jurisdictions analysed, credit institutions – i.e., in principle banks – retain a central role in credit distribution, either through direct lending or via structured networks of credit intermediaries. However, national regulations differ significantly to the extent that banks rely on third-party intermediaries. In some countries, intermediaries operate primarily as external channels through which banks expand their distribution capacity, especially in underserved or niche markets. In others, they assume a more autonomous advisory role, sometimes with stricter limitations to ensure lender independence. These aspects between credit institutions and intermediaries are affected by the legal definitions, licensing regimes and supervisory expectations found in each country. Through the examination of these relationships, the book tries to clarify how intermediaries, such as agents and brokers, act as extensions of the banking system with their own regulatory obligations and market strategies.

REGULATORY FRAMEWORKS FOR CREDIT INTERMEDIARIES IN EUROPE

The regulation of credit intermediaries in Europe is characterised by a high degree of diversity, reflecting specific legal and market conditions in each jurisdiction. While the European Union has sought to harmonise certain aspects of credit intermediation through directives, such as the MCD and the CCD, significant differences remain in how member states implement these regulations. Over the past two decades, the European Union has progressively developed a regulatory framework for credit agreements with consumers, aiming to ensure a high level of consumer protection, enhance the functioning of the internal market and promote financial stability. Two key legislative acts of the European Parliament and the Council have emerged from this effort: the CCD (Directive 2008/48/EC, CCD) and the MCD (Directive 2014/17/EU, MCD). These directives were introduced in response to growing concerns about asymmetries in consumer protection across Member States, a lack of transparency in credit agreements and divergent national approaches that hindered cross-border activity in retail financial services.

Both these Directives are in force as repeatedly amended. It is worth noting that in 2023, the European Parliament and the Council adopted a new CCD (Directive (EU) 2023/225, CCD2), which repeals and replaces the existing EU consumer credit regime. Member States are required to transpose this new legislative act by 20 November 2025 and apply the new measures from 20 November 2026. The study at hand does not deal with that legislative act.

The CCD, adopted in 2008, addressed the need to harmonise the national rules applicable to unsecured consumer credit, ensuring that consumers throughout the EU receive standardised, comparable information before entering into a credit agreement. The MCD, adopted after the (2007–2009) global financial crisis, was part of a broader policy initiative to foster responsible lending and borrowing in the markets for mortgage lending – areas that had shown significant regulatory gaps and risks for household over-indebtedness. Both directives have not only established baseline consumer rights and obligations for credit providers and intermediaries, but have also reshaped national regulatory landscapes by imposing shared definitions, disclosure obligations, professional standards and conduct rules.

While both directives leave room for national discretion and interpretation – particularly in the case of the MCD, which allows stricter national rules – they have significantly influenced the structure, supervision and legal status of credit intermediaries across Europe. Understanding the core features and policy logic of the CCD and MCD is therefore essential for appreciating the similarities and divergences that characterise national frameworks, and for evaluating the extent to which EU-level harmonisation has been effective or fragmented in practice.

This topic in the study provides an overview of the regulatory frameworks governing credit intermediaries in the seven jurisdictions covered by this study: Belgium, France, Germany, Italy, Spain, Portugal and the United Kingdom.

In Belgium, credit intermediaries are subject to a structured regulatory framework that includes licensing requirements, professional standards and ongoing supervision. The Belgian Financial Services and Markets Authority (FSMA) is responsible for overseeing the activities of credit intermediaries, ensuring that they comply with legal and professional standards. Credit intermediaries in Belgium must demonstrate their trustworthiness, financial stability and competence in order to obtain a license. They are also required to adhere to high standards of professional conduct, including obligations to act in the best interests of their clients and provide transparent and accurate information.

In France, credit intermediaries are regulated by the French Prudential Supervision and Resolution Authority (ACPR), the General Directorate for Competition, Consumer Affairs and Fraud Control (DGCCRF) and the ORIAS. The regulatory framework in France is characterised by a high degree of consumer protection, with stringent requirements for transparency, disclosure and professional conduct. Credit intermediaries in France must obtain a license, which involves demonstrating their financial stability, competence and adherence to professional standards. They are also required to provide clients with clear and comprehensive information about the credit products they offer, including any fees or commissions.

In Germany, credit intermediaries are supervised by Trade Supervisory Authorities of the federal state level (Bundesländer). The regulatory framework in Germany emphasises the importance of consumer protection and market integrity. In general, all credit intermediaries are required to act honestly, fairly and professionally in the best interests of their clients. They must possess adequate knowledge and competence in credit intermediation and credit products, supported by appropriate education and training. When providing advice, intermediaries must ensure that it is objective, tailored to the customer's profile and proportionate to the complexity of the products and the associated risks.

In Italy, credit intermediaries are regulated by the OAM – Organismo Agenti e Mediatori, under the supervision of the Bank of Italy. The regulatory framework in Italy is characterised by a relatively very high degree of consumer protection, with stringent requirements for transparency, disclosure and professional conduct. Credit intermediaries in Italy must obtain a license from the OAM, which involves demonstrating that they meet licensing requirements, competence and adherence to professional standards. Also, in this case, they are required to provide clients with clear and comprehensive information about the credit products they offer, including any fees or commissions.

In Spain, credit intermediaries are regulated under different frameworks depending on the type of credit involved. Real estate credit intermediaries, as defined by Law 5/2019, must register with the Bank of Spain, while consumer credit intermediaries, under Law 16/2011, are not subject to licensing or registration requirements unless they also operate as real estate credit intermediaries. Additionally, Circular 4/2021 of the Bank of Spain mandates that institutions under its supervision, including credit institutions and certain financial entities, report biannually on their appointed agents, a role distinct from intermediaries. These agents act on behalf of supervised entities and are subject to oversight to ensure compliance with transparency and consumer protection obligations, which involves demonstrating their trustworthiness, financial stability and competence. Credit intermediaries are required to adhere to high standards of professional conduct, including obligations to act in the best interests of their clients and provide transparent and accurate information.

In Portugal, credit intermediaries are regulated under Decree-Law No. 81-C/2017, with oversight from the Bank of Portugal. The regulatory framework ensures consumer protection by imposing strict requirements on transparency, disclosure and professional conduct. Credit intermediaries must obtain authorisation from the Bank of Portugal, demonstrating compliance with financial, organisational and competency requirements.

They are classified into three categories: tied intermediaries, ancillary intermediaries and untied intermediaries, each subject to distinct regulatory obligations. Tied and ancillary intermediaries can only receive compensation from lenders, whereas untied intermediaries are remunerated solely by consumers. The framework also establishes prohibitions against misleading advertising, unauthorised advisory services and improper remuneration practices, ensuring that credit intermediation operates with integrity and consumer confidence.

In the United Kingdom, credit intermediaries are regulated by the FCA. The regulatory framework in the UK is characterised by a high degree of consumer protection, with stringent requirements for transparency, disclosure and professional conduct. Credit intermediaries in the UK must obtain authorisation from the FCA to carry out permitted activities. This involves demonstrating their financial stability, competence and adherence to professional standards. They are also required to provide consumers with clear and comprehensive information about the credit products they offer, including any fees or commissions.

Licensing Requirements for Credit Intermediaries

Requirements are designed to protect consumers, maintain market integrity and promote financial stability. Licensing requirements help to prevent fraud, mismanagement and other risks that could harm consumers or destabilise the financial system; in addition, they set clear standards for entry into the market. This section delves deeper into the national licensing requirements, their key components and their broader implications for the entities active in the sector.

One of the primary reasons for licensing requirements is to safeguard consumers. Credit intermediaries facilitate access to credit, which often involves significant financial decisions for individuals and businesses. Without proper oversight, intermediaries could engage in unethical practices, such as mis-selling products, charging hidden fees or providing misleading information. Licensing requirements ensure that intermediaries meet minimum standards of competence, professionalism and ethical conduct. For example, intermediaries are typically required to demonstrate a thorough understanding of credit products, regulatory obligations and risk management practices. This ensures that they can provide accurate and objective advice to consumers, and it helps them make informed decisions.

Moreover, licensing requirements often include provisions for transparency and disclosure. Intermediaries must disclose their fees, commissions and any potential conflicts of interest, such as affiliations with specific credit providers. This transparency helps consumers understand the true cost of credit and the motivations behind the advice they receive. By holding intermediaries accountable to these standards, licensing requirements reduce the risk of consumer harm and build trust in the financial system.

Licensing requirements also contribute to maintaining market integrity and stability. Credit intermediaries operate at the intersection of borrowers and lenders, and they facilitate the flow of credit that underpins economic activity. If intermediaries are not properly regulated, they could engage in risky or fraudulent practices that undermine market confidence. For instance, an unlicensed intermediary might facilitate loans to uncreditworthy borrowers, increasing the risk of defaults and financial instability. Licensing requirements help mitigate these risks by ensuring that intermediaries have the necessary financial resources, organisational structure and risk management systems in place.

In addition, licensing requirements often include ongoing supervision and compliance obligations. Regulatory authorities monitor licensed intermediaries to ensure they continue to meet the required standards throughout their operations. This ongoing oversight helps to identify and address potential issues before they escalate into systemic risks. For example, if an intermediary is found to be engaging in predatory lending practices, regulators can take corrective action, such as revoking their license or imposing fines. This proactive approach helps to maintain the integrity of the credit market and prevent broader financial instability.

Another key aspect of licensing requirements is the emphasis on professional standards and competence. Credit intermediation is a complex field that requires specialised knowledge and skills. Intermediaries must understand the intricacies of credit products, regulatory frameworks and risk assessment techniques. Licensing requirements ensure that intermediaries possess the necessary expertise by mandating specific qualifications, training and experience. For example, in many jurisdictions, intermediaries must pass rigorous exams or complete accredited training programs before they can obtain a license.

These requirements also extend to the organisational level. Intermediaries must demonstrate that they have robust internal controls, compliance systems and governance structures in place. This ensures that they can manage risks effectively and operate in a manner that is consistent with legal and professional standards. Then, setting high standards for competence and professionalism, it allows for building licensing requirements that help to elevate the quality of services provided by intermediaries, benefiting both consumers and the broader financial system.

Licensing requirements also serve as a barrier to entry, ensuring that only serious and credible players can operate in the market. This helps to prevent the proliferation of unqualified or fraudulent intermediaries, which could undermine consumer confidence and market stability. At the same time, licensing requirements promote market discipline by creating a level playing field for all participants. Licensed intermediaries are held to the same standards, regardless of their size or market share. This fosters healthy competition and encourages intermediaries to differentiate themselves based on the quality of their services rather than engaging in unethical practices.

In the context of the European Union, licensing requirements also play a role in promoting cross-border consistency and harmonisation. While each member state has its own regulatory framework, EU directives could help to establish common standards for credit intermediation. Licensing requirements help to ensure that intermediaries operating across borders meet these common standards, facilitating market integration and reducing regulatory arbitrage. This is particularly important in a single market like the EU, where intermediaries often operate in multiple jurisdictions.

CHALLENGES AND OPPORTUNITIES FOR CREDIT INTERMEDIARIES IN EUROPE

The regulatory environment for credit intermediaries in Europe is both complex and diversified, presenting a range of challenges and opportunities. This study helps to explore some of the key challenges faced by credit intermediaries, as well as the opportunities for innovation and growth in the sector, by comparing different country-level circumstances.

One of the primary challenges for credit intermediaries is facing the fragmented regulatory landscape in Europe. While the European Union has sought to harmonise certain aspects of credit intermediation through directives such as the MCD and the CCD, significant differences remain in how member states implement these regulations. This creates a challenging environment for credit intermediaries operating across multiple jurisdictions, as they must comply with a diverse range of legal and professional standards.

Another challenge for credit intermediaries is managing conflicts of interest. Credit intermediaries can receive commissions or other forms of remuneration from credit providers, which can create incentives to prioritise the interests of lenders over those of borrowers. Regulatory frameworks in Europe seek to address this issue by imposing strict transparency and disclosure requirements, but conflicts of interest remain a significant concern. Credit intermediaries must navigate these challenges carefully, ensuring that they act in the best interests of their clients while maintaining their financial capability.

Technological change is another major challenge for credit intermediaries. The rise of fintech and digital platforms has transformed the way credit is distributed, creating new opportunities for innovation but also disrupting traditional business models. Credit intermediaries must adapt to these changes by adopting new technologies and developing new skills. At the same time, they must ensure that they comply with regulatory requirements, which can be particularly challenging in the fast-moving fintech sector.

Despite these challenges, there are also significant opportunities for credit intermediaries in Europe. A growing demand for credit presents a major opportunity for growth. Credit intermediaries can capitalise on this demand by expanding their product offerings and improving their service delivery. In addition, the increasing focus on financial inclusion presents an opportunity for credit intermediaries to reach underserved markets and promote responsible lending practices.

This study provides a comprehensive overview of the regulatory frameworks governing credit intermediaries in Europe, offering insights for policymakers, regulators and industry stakeholders.

Open Access This chapter is licensed under the terms of the Creative Commons Attribution 4.0 International License (http://creativecommons.org/licenses/by/4.0/), which permits use, sharing, adaptation, distribution and reproduction in any medium or format, as long as you give appropriate credit to the original author(s) and the source, provide a link to the Creative Commons license and indicate if changes were made.

The images or other third party material in this chapter are included in the chapter's Creative Commons license, unless indicated otherwise in a credit line to the material. If material is not included in the chapter's Creative Commons license and your intended use is not permitted by statutory regulation or exceeds the permitted use, you will need to obtain permission directly from the copyright holder.

CHAPTER 2

Belgium

Abstract This chapter examines the Belgian credit intermediation sector, focusing on its regulatory framework, licensing requirements, and supervisory authorities. It analyzes the role of the Financial Services and Markets Authority (FSMA) and the Federal Public Service Finances (FPS - Service public fédéral Finances). Particular attention is given to the licensing system under Belgian law, the distinction between mortgage and consumer credit intermediation, and transparency obligations toward consumers. The chapter also discusses the evolution of regulatory oversight and challenges linked to compliance costs and digitalization.

Keywords Belgium • credit intermediaries • FSMA • FPS • mortgage credit • consumer credit • licensing • supervision

The regulatory framework for credit intermediation in Belgium is governed by a combination of national laws and directives transposed from the European Union. Credit intermediaries facilitate access to credit for both consumers and businesses, and their operations are supervised primarily by the FSMA. Licensing requirements, categorisation of intermediaries and their compliance obligations are strictly defined by Belgian legislation. This chapter explores the typology of intermediaries, the procedures for authorisation and the applicable prudential and conduct rules.

CREDIT INTERMEDIARIES IN BELGIUM

In Belgium, the regulation of credit intermediaries is governed by the Code of Economic Law (CEL). It ensures that both mortgage and consumer credit intermediaries operate within a structured legal framework. To protect consumers and maintain market integrity, intermediaries must comply with strict registration requirements set by the FSMA. This framework categorises intermediaries into distinct groups, each with specific roles and responsibilities. Understanding these categories and the associated regulations is needed to ensure compliance and to protect consumer interests.

Definition of Credit Intermediary

According to Belgian law[1], a "credit intermediary" is defined as a legal person or a natural person who is self-employed within the meaning of social legislation. These individuals or entities do not act as creditors themselves but, during their commercial or professional activities, for remuneration which may be pecuniary or take any other form of agreed economic advantage, carry out credit intermediation activities. This definition also includes those who offer or grant credit agreements, where these agreements are immediately assigned or subrogated in favour of another approved or registered creditor designated in the agreement.

Credit intermediaries are required to deal only with companies or persons authorised or registered to carry out credit activities in Belgium. They must also sign up for an out-of-court settlement mechanism for consumer disputes and provide the FSMA with a professional email address for official communications.

According to Article VII.177 of CEL, credit intermediaries are categorised into two main types:

1. mortgage credit intermediaries;
2. consumer credit intermediaries.

[1] Art. I.9 35° Book VII of the Code of Economic Law

A "mortgage credit intermediary" refers to intermediaries operating within the mortgage credit sector, while a "consumer credit intermediary" refers to intermediaries active in the consumer credit sector.

Mortgage credit intermediaries, according to Article VII.180 of CEL, are divided into the following categories:

1. credit brokers;
2. tied agents;
3. subagents.

Mortgage credit intermediaries must appoint one or more natural persons responsible for distribution. The number of responsible individuals must be appropriate to the intermediary's organisation and its activities. Mortgage credit intermediaries must report periodically to the FSMA, providing an updated list of distribution managers and noting any changes to this list. They must keep available the FSMA documents verifying the professional qualifications of both the distribution managers and other employees interacting with the public.

According to Article VII.185, Credit intermediaries in the consumer credit sector are divided into:

1. credit brokers;
2. tied agents;
3. ancillary agents.

Consumer credit intermediaries must designate one or more natural persons responsible for distribution. The number of these responsible individuals should correspond to the organisational structure and scope of activities of the intermediary. These credit intermediaries must report periodically to the FSMA on the implementation of this obligation, submitting the list of the responsible persons for distribution, as well as details of any changes made to this list. Intermediaries are required to keep documents demonstrating the professional qualifications of both the responsible persons and individuals in direct contact with the public available for the FSMA.

No one may assume the title of mortgage credit intermediary or any of its subdivisions, which would imply participation in mortgage credit intermediary activities as outlined in this section, unless they are registered in the appropriate FSMA registry.

1. Credit Brokers – Definition of a "Credit Broker"
   A credit broker is a type of intermediary who, unlike tied agents or subagents, conducts credit intermediation independently[2], without being bound by an exclusive agency agreement or any other legal obligation to place all or a portion of their production with a specific lender or a set of lenders[3].
2. Tied Agents – Definition of a "Tied Agent"
   A tied agent is a credit intermediary who operates on behalf of and under the full responsibility of either[4]:
   (a) a single lender, or
   (b) multiple lenders belonging to the same group.
3. Ancillary Agents – Definition of an "Ancillary Agent."

An ancillary agent is a credit intermediary whose primary business involves the sale of non-financial goods and services, and who acts as a credit intermediary on behalf of one or more credit institutions[5].

Ancillary agents are classified into two types:

- those whose offered credit is solely intended for goods and services they themselves sell;
- those whose offered credit can also be used for goods and services not sold by the agent.

Credit Intermediary and Licensing Requirements for Credit Intermediaries

As said, in Belgium, the legal framework for credit intermediaries is defined and regulated to ensure that parties involved in the credit distribution sector operate under guidelines that protect both consumers and the integrity of the financial system. The framework is established under the CEL, which provides detailed regulations for obtaining licenses and the

---

[2] A credit broker must declare, under oath, that they are not exclusively tied to a particular creditor and that they are under no obligation to direct their production to a specific creditor or group of lenders. If a broker becomes exclusively bound to a single entity or required to allocate their production to one or more companies in the same group, they must immediately cease intermediary activities and notify the FSMA.

[3] https://www.fsma.be/fr/intermediaires-preteurs/quest-ce-quun-courtier-de-credit

[4] https://www.fsma.be/fr/intermediaires-preteurs/quest-ce-quun-agent-lie

[5] https://www.fsma.be/fr/intermediaires-preteurs/quest-ce-quun-agent-titre-accessoire

operation of credit intermediaries, including credit brokers, tied agents and accessory agents.

Considering Mortgage Credit Intermediaries, the CEL[6] specifies that mortgage credit intermediaries whose home Member State is Belgium cannot operate unless they are first entered in the register maintained by the FSMA.

Mortgage credit intermediaries must possess the professional knowledge determined by Royal Decree. They must also demonstrate sufficient appropriate expertise and professional integrity to carry out their duties effectively. This includes having the necessary qualifications and experience to understand and manage the complexities of mortgage credit products and services.[7]

Mortgage credit intermediaries must be covered by professional indemnity insurance. This insurance protects against claims arising from professional negligence or misconduct, ensuring that intermediaries can meet potential liabilities that might arise from their business activities.

Applicants for registration as mortgage credit brokers must attach a declaration stating that they conduct their professional activities without any exclusive agency agreements or legal commitments requiring them to place all or part of their production with specific lenders. This ensures that brokers can offer impartial advice and services to consumers.

When the credit intermediary is a legal entity, additional requirements apply. The members of the administrative body, as well as the individuals entrusted with the effective management of the entity, must possess the professional knowledge, expertise and good repute necessary to perform their duties. The FSMA must be notified of the identity of the shareholders controlling the company, and these shareholders must have the qualities necessary to guarantee sound and prudent management.

To summarise, the conditions that have to be met are the following[8]:

1. have the professional knowledge determined by Royal Decree;
2. have sufficient appropriate expertise and professional integrity to carry out their duties;
3. mortgage credit intermediation must be covered by professional indemnity insurance;

---

[6] Art. VII.180 – Code of Economic Law
[7] Art. VII.181 – Code of Economic Law
[8] *Ibidem*

4. deal only with companies or persons who, pursuant to the CEL, are authorised or registered to carry on this activity in Belgium;
5. sign up for an out-of-court settlement of consumer disputes;
6. pay the fees due to FSMA for carrying out the audit;
7. provide FSMA with a professional e-mail address to which FSMA may validly send all communications;
8. mortgage credit intermediaries must demonstrate to FSMA, in accordance with the rules specified by the latter by way of regulation, including with regard to periodicity, compliance with the provisions;
9. applicants for registration as mortgage credit brokers must attach to their application for registration a declaration on their honour stating that they carry out their professional activities without any exclusive agency agreement or any other legal commitment requiring them to place all or a specific part of their production with one or more lenders.

When it concerns a legal person, additionally:

1. The members of the administrative body, as well as the persons entrusted with the effective management of this legal person, must possess the professional knowledge determined by Royal Decree, as well as adequate expertise and sufficient good repute to perform their duties.
2. The legal entity notifies FSMA of the identity of the shareholders controlling the company; these shareholders must, in FSMA's judgement, have the necessary qualities with regard to the need to guarantee sound and prudent management.

Considering Consumer Credit Intermediaries, Articles VII.184 and subsequent sections of the CEL specify similar conditions for consumer credit intermediaries. These intermediaries are categorised into **Credit Brokers, Tied Agents** and **Accessory Agents**[9].

These intermediaries must comply with the relevant professional knowledge, expertise and integrity requirements, ensuring that they operate within the regulatory framework designed to protect consumers and maintain market stability.

---

[9] Article VII.185 of the Code of Economic Law

To be registered in the register of intermediaries in *consumer credit*, and to maintain this registration, the applicant for registration as a broker or tied agent must meet the following conditions[10]:

1. the intermediary, the persons responsible for distribution, and those in contact with the public must possess the professional knowledge determined by the King;
2. the intermediary and the persons responsible for distribution must possess adequate expertise and sufficient professional integrity to perform their tasks;
3. the activity of consumer credit intermediation must be covered by professional liability insurance, covering the entire territory of the European Economic Area. The insurance contract must include a clause obliging the insurance company, upon termination of the contract, to notify the FSMA. The King, upon advice from the FSMA, sets the conditions for this insurance;
4. with regard to their activity as a consumer credit intermediary in Belgium, they may only deal with companies or persons who are authorised or registered to carry out this activity in Belgium;
5. they must adhere to an out-of-court consumer dispute resolution scheme as referred to in Article VII.216, contribute to the financing of this scheme and respond to any request for information made in connection with the handling of complaints through this scheme;
6. they must pay the fees owed to the FSMA for the purpose of supervision;
7. they must provide the FSMA with a professional email address, to which the FSMA can validly send all communications, whether individual or collective.

In addition, if a *legal entity* applies for registration as an intermediary, the following provisions shall apply:

1. the persons entrusted with the effective management of this legal entity must possess the professional knowledge determined by the King, as well as adequate expertise and sufficient professional integrity to perform their tasks.
2. The legal entity must communicate to the FSMA the identity of the shareholders holding control of the company; these shareholders must, in the FSMA's judgement, possess the necessary qualities with

---

[10] Art. VII.186 of the Code of Economic Law

regard to ensuring sound and prudent management. Any change in the identity of shareholders holding control must be communicated to the FSMA.

An applicant for registration as a *broker in consumer credit* must attach to their application a statement indicating that they carry out their professional activities independently of any exclusive agency contract or other legal commitment requiring them to place all or a determined part of their production.

Any changes to the data covered by the sworn statement referred to in the first paragraph must be communicated to the FSMA without delay.

A *tied agent* acts, with regard to their consumer credit intermediation activity, under the full and unconditional responsibility of the consumer credit lender(s) on whose behalf they act. The applicant for registration as a tied agent must establish this in their registration file.

The lender(s) must control the compliance of the tied agent with the provisions of this book and the decrees and regulations issued in execution thereof.

The procedure to apply for registration as a broker, tied agent and ancillary agents is specified on the FSMA website[11].

Laws and Relevant Authorities in Belgium

In Belgium, the regulation and supervision of credit intermediaries are overseen by two principal authorities: the FSMA and the FPS (Federal Public Service Finances).

The FSMA is a main actor in the registration procedures necessary for obtaining accreditation. All credit intermediaries must secure accreditation from the FSMA to operate legally. This process ensures that all credit intermediaries meet stringent criteria designed to maintain the integrity and stability of the financial market. The FSMA's regulatory framework encompasses aspects of financial operations that ensure accredited entities adhere to high standards of professionalism, transparency and consumer protection. In addition to the FSMA, the FPS is responsible for ensuring compliance with credit legislation. This involves supervising credit providers to ensure they adhere to the legal requirements governing credit activities in Belgium. The economic inspection arm of the FPS conducts regular controls and

---

[11] https://www.fsma.be/fr/intermediaires-preteurs

audits to verify that all credit providers operate within the legal framework. This includes monitoring their business practices, verifying their adherence to consumer protection laws and ensuring they maintain fair and transparent operations. Both regulatory bodies collaborate to supervise the financial system. While the FSMA focuses on the accreditation and ongoing regulatory compliance of financial intermediaries, the FPS ensures that these entities comply with the broader credit legislation. This dual oversight mechanism helps maintain a robust and fair financial system, protecting consumers and promoting confidence in the financial market.

Credit providers, after obtaining accreditation from the FSMA, are subject to the same legislative requirements and controls by the FPS Economy. This uniformity in regulatory expectations ensures that all credit providers, regardless of their nature, are held to the same high standards of conduct and rules.

The main laws and regulations governing credit distribution activities include:

- Code of Economic Law, Book VII: this is the primary legal text that outlines the rules and obligations for credit distribution. It covers various aspects of economic activity, including consumer protection and the responsibilities of credit providers and intermediaries.
- Royal Decree of 29 October 2015: This decree implements Title 4, Chapter 4, of Book VII of the Code of Economic Law. It provides detailed regulations and guidelines for the execution of credit-related activities, ensuring that all procedures comply with the overarching economic law[12].

On 24 December 2021, the Belgian Royal Decree of 12 December 2021, titled "Harmonising Several Royal Decrees on Mediation in the Financial and Insurance Sectors" (the "Harmonization Royal Decree"), was published in the Belgian State Gazette. This decree standardises the legal status and registration requirements for intermediaries across three main sectors: (i) banking and investment services, (ii) consumer and mortgage credit and (iii) insurance. The new regulations came into effect on 1 January 2022, with transitional measures in place to facilitate compliance. Principal changes for intermediaries in consumer and mortgage credit include clarified professional knowledge requirements (with exemptions

---

[12] French version: Arrêté Royal du 29/10/2015 portant exécution du titre 4, chapitre 4, du livre VII du code de droit économique

for certain degrees), mandatory continuous training and professional liability insurance. Credit intermediaries must also disclose AML/CFT compliance officers and notify the FSMA if liability insurance lapses.

- Royal Decree Regulating the Spread of the Commission for Mediation on Credit Agreements: Issued on 7 December 2016, this decree regulates how commissions for mediation on credit agreements are to be distributed. It aims to ensure that commissions are paid in a manner that promotes fairness and transparency in the credit mediation process[13].

Open Access This chapter is licensed under the terms of the Creative Commons Attribution 4.0 International License (http://creativecommons.org/licenses/by/4.0/), which permits use, sharing, adaptation, distribution and reproduction in any medium or format, as long as you give appropriate credit to the original author(s) and the source, provide a link to the Creative Commons license and indicate if changes were made.

The images or other third party material in this chapter are included in the chapter's Creative Commons license, unless indicated otherwise in a credit line to the material. If material is not included in the chapter's Creative Commons license and your intended use is not permitted by statutory regulation or exceeds the permitted use, you will need to obtain permission directly from the copyright holder.

---

[13] French version: Arrêté Royal du 07/12/2016 réglementant l'échelonnement de la commission pour l'intervention des intermédiaires en matière de contrats de crédit

CHAPTER 3

France

Abstract This chapter explores the French regulatory and market framework for credit intermediaries. It outlines the French legal provisions regulating financial agents and brokers and highlights the role of ORIAS (Organization for the Register of Insurance, Banking and Finance Intermediaries) and the ACPR (*Autorité de contrôle prudentiel et de résolution*). The chapter discusses the licensing requirements, including competence and transparency obligations. It highlights France's emphasis on consumer protection, the role of professional conduct codes, and the structure of the domestic law.

Keywords France • ORIAS • ACPR • credit brokers • financial agents • consumer protection • licensing requirements • EU directives

Credit intermediation in France is principally governed by the *Code monétaire et financier* and overseen by the *Autorité de Contrôle Prudentiel et de Résolution* (ACPR). Credit brokers and intermediaries (*Intermédiaires en Opérations de Banque et en Services de Paiement* – IOBSP) must adhere to licensing, registration and conduct rules. The chapter provides an overview of the licensing requirements and institutional roles. Notably, the ASF represents and coordinates non-bank credit institutions and financial institutions. This section maps the regulatory regime, with attention to the professional obligations and the enforcement mechanisms applicable to French intermediaries.

CREDIT INTERMEDIARIES IN FRANCE

Intermediation in banking transactions and payment services in France is defined as the activity of presenting, proposing, or assisting in the conclusion of banking transactions or payment services[1]. This activity also includes performing any preparatory work or advisory services necessary for their execution. In addition, intermediaries in banking operations and payment services ("intermédiaires en opérations de banque et en services de paiement," henceforth "IOBSP") are defined as any person who seeks or obtains the client's consent for a banking transaction or payment service, or explains orally or in writing the terms and conditions of a banking transaction or payment service to a potential client, and/or presenting, proposing or assisting in the conclusion of a banking transaction or the provision of a payment service for its design or delivery.

According to the *Code Monétaire et Financier*[2], there are four categories of IOBSP:

1. **The broker in banking operations and payment services**: these are registered in the Trade and Companies Register for the purpose of intermediation in banking operations and payment services. They act as intermediaries on behalf of the client, excluding any mandate from a credit institution, financial company, payment institution, e-money institution providing payment services, crowdfunding intermediary, insurance company within the scope of its lending activities, or management company within the scope of its FIA management activities[3]. They are not contractually obligated to work exclusively with a credit institution, financial company, payment institution, e-money institution providing payment services, crowdfunding intermediary, insurance company within the scope of its lending activities or management company within the scope of its FIA management activities[4].

---

[1] According to Article L519-1 of the French Monetary and Financial Code
[2] Art. L. 519-4 – Monetary and Financial Code
[3] Art. L. 511-6
[4] Art. L. 511-6 (Art. 519-4-1-1°)

2. **The exclusive agent in banking operations and payment services:** these intermediaries act under a mandate from a credit institution, financial company, payment institution, e-money institution providing payment services, crowdfunding intermediary or insurance company within the scope of its activities, or a management company within the scope of its FIA management activities[5]. They are contractually obligated to work exclusively with one of these entities for a specific category of banking operations or payment services[6]
3. **The non-exclusive agent in banking operations and payment services:** these intermediaries act under one or more non-exclusive mandates issued by one or more credit institutions, financial companies, payment institutions, e-money institutions providing payment services, crowdfunding intermediaries, insurance companies within the scope of their lending activities or management companies within the scope of their FIA management activities[7]
4. **The agent of an intermediary in banking operations and payment services:** these intermediaries act under a mandate from the individuals referred to in points 1, 2 or 3, as well as from individuals mentioned in point III who operate under the freedom to provide services and freedom of establishment within French territory[8].

Among the activities that brokers carry out, they can provide advisory services that involve offering clients, including potential clients, personalised recommendations regarding one or more operations related to credit agreements. This activity is distinct from the granting of credit and the intermediation of banking operations and payment services.

These personalised recommendations pertain to one or more credit agreements tailored to the needs and financial situation of the client, taking into account:

- a sufficiently large number of credit agreements within their range of products for intermediaries acting under a mandate issued by a credit institution or a financial company; or

---

[5] Art. L. 511-6
[6] Art. R. 519-4-1-2°
[7] Art L. 511-6. (Art. R519-4-1-3°)
[8] Art. R. 519-4-1-4°

- a sufficiently large number of credit agreements available in the market for intermediaries acting under a mandate issued by a client.

Advice is considered independent when it is based on a sufficiently large number of credit agreements available in the market and when its provision does not result in any remuneration other than that paid, if applicable, by the client, nor in any other form of economic benefit.

A credit intermediary providing independent advisory services may claim the title of "independent advisor."

The conditions for providing advisory services are specified by a decree of the Conseil d'État.

Regarding exceptions, this article 519-1 doesn't apply to:

- credit institutions.
- Financing companies.
- Portfolio management companies managing collective investments.
- Electronic money institutions providing payment services.
- Payment institutions and account information service providers.
- Employees of the aforementioned entities.
- Persons engaged in intermediation activities who meet specific conditions set by a **decree in the Council of State** based on the intermediary's activity and the type of credit or payment service contract.

The activity of acting as an IOBSP may only be carried out between two parties, at least one of which is a credit institution, a finance company, an electronic money institution providing payment services, a payment institution, a crowdfunding intermediary, a crowdfunding service provider in the context of its loan facilitation activities, an insurance undertaking in the context of its lending activities, or an asset management company in the context of its management of alternative investment fund[9].

The IOBSP acts under a mandate issued by one or more of the companies mentioned above. However, by way of derogation and under conditions fixed by a decree in the Council of State, the intermediary in banking and payment services transactions may act under a mandate issued by another intermediary in banking and payment services transactions or by the client. The mandate under which the intermediary in banking and payment services transactions acts specifies the nature and conditions of the transactions that he is authorised to carry out.

---

[9] Article L519-2

A transaction concluded in the context of one of the activities mentioned may not be intermediated consecutively by: 1° More than two intermediaries in banking and payment services transactions; 2° More than one intermediary in banking and payment services transactions when the latter has put its client in touch with a crowdfunding intermediary or a crowdfunding service provider in the context of its loan facilitation activities under the conditions provided for in this article.

The remuneration, as referred to in paragraph I of Article L. 519-1, shall be understood as any monetary payment or any other form of economic benefit agreed upon and linked to the intermediation service. The remuneration granted for intermediation activity may only be paid, in whole or in part, to one of the intermediaries mentioned in Article R. 519-4-1. The conditions or level of remuneration received by IOBSP for their intermediation activities, as well as the methods by which intermediaries in banking and payment services remunerate their staff, must not conflict with the obligation to act in the best interests of clients or compromise the quality of service provision.

When IOBSP provide an advisory service as defined in Article L. 519-1-1, the remuneration of its staff for such services must not depend solely on sales targets[10].

Before concluding any banking transaction or payment service or any preparatory work and consultancy, the intermediary must agree with his client, including any potential client, in writing or on another durable medium, any commissions and, where applicable, the remuneration that will be due to him[11].

It is prohibited for any individual or entity, in any capacity or by any means, whether directly or indirectly, to collect any amount representing advance payments, commissions, research fees, administrative fees, or any other intermediary charges before the actual disbursement of loaned funds.

As an exception to Article L. 519-6, and within the framework of providing independent advisory services as defined in Article L. 519-1-1, banking and payment service intermediaries may receive remuneration directly from their clients[12]. The remuneration allocated for intermediation activity must only be paid, in whole or in part, to one of the intermediaries mentioned in paragraph 1° or 3° of Article R. 519-4[13].

---

[10] Article R519-25
[11] Art. R519-26
[12] Article L519-6-1
[13] Article L519-5-2

Credit Intermediary and Licensing Requirements for Credit Intermediaries

IOBSP must be registered in a register of intermediaries (ORIAS[14]). To register, they must meet a certain number of conditions, such as good reputation, professional capacity and professional insurance in certain cases. These requirements vary, depending on whether the intermediary is a broker (acting on behalf of the client, consumer or company), or an agent (acting on behalf of the credit institution or financing company), and for agents, whether they offer consumer credit as an accessory to their main activity.

It should also be noted that for certain consumer credits, intermediaries acting in an ancillary capacity are only required to register with ORIAS if their credit activity exceeds thresholds in terms of amount and number of transactions.

The ORIAS registration process is designed to ensure that only qualified and trustworthy intermediaries are permitted to operate in the market. The ORIAS helps to protect consumers from fraud, misconduct and other forms of financial harm, and it imposes rigorous requirements and conducts regular inspections. Moreover, by maintaining a register of authorised intermediaries, ORIAS facilitates market transparency and enables regulatory authorities to identify and address potential risks.

To register, IOBSP must meet a certain number of conditions (good repute, professional capacity and professional insurance in certain cases). These requirements vary depending on whether the intermediary is:

- a broker, acting on behalf of the client, consumer or company;
- or an agent, acting on behalf of the credit institution or financing company;
- and for agents, whether they offer consumer credit as an accessory to their main activity (case of the vast majority of intermediaries mandated by ASF[15] members).

---

[14] ORIAS is the body in charge of the Official Register of Insurance, Banking and Finance Intermediaries, under the supervision of the General Directorate of the Treasury (Ministry of Economy). The registration of these intermediaries on this Register is mandatory. The Orias website allows you to verify that the intermediary is authorised to distribute insurance, banking or financial products.

[15] Association française des Sociétés Financières (ASF)

It should also be noted that for certain consumer credits, intermediaries acting in an ancillary capacity are only required to register with ORIAS if their credit activity exceeds thresholds in terms of amount and number of transactions.

The scope of ORIAS' mission was extended in 2010[16] to IOBSP, as well as to financial investment advisors and tied agents for investment services.

In particular, as specified before, according to the Code monétaire et financier[17], there are four categories of IOBSP:

1. the broker in banking operations and payment services[18];
2. the exclusive agent in banking operations and payment services[19];
3. the non-exclusive agent in banking operations and payment services[20];
4. the agent of an intermediary in banking operations and payment services[21].

Requirements for broker (R. 519-4-1-1°), non-exclusive agent (R. 519-4-1-3°) and for their representatives (Agent of an intermediary in banking operations and payment services according to R. 519-4-1-4°).

IOBSP mentioned under point 1° of paragraph I of Article R. 519-4, their representatives under point 4° of the same paragraph, as well as those referred to under point 3° of paragraph I of Article R. 519-4 and their representatives, must provide evidence of professional competence demonstrated through[22]:

1. diploma certifying higher education at level 6 of the national qualifications framework;
2. 150 hours of professional training relevant to banking operations or payment services, completed with:
   (a) a credit institution, financial company, payment institution, e-money institution providing payment services, insurance company or intermediary in banking operations and payment services

---

[16] Loi de régulation bancaire et financière n°2010–1249 du 22 octobre 2010.
[17] Art. L519-4
[18] Art. 519-4-1-1°
[19] Art. R519-4-1-2°
[20] Art. R519-4-1-3°
[21] Art. R519-4-1-4°
[22] Art. R519-8

as defined in paragraph I of this article, different from the entity where such intermediaries operate;
(b) a training organisation chosen by the individual, their employer or, if applicable, their principal, under the conditions stipulated in Article R. 519-12.

By way of derogation, intermediaries are considered to have professional competence when they can demonstrate:

1. one year of professional experience in functions related to banking operations or payment services acquired in the three years prior to registration in the unified register referred to in Article L. 546-1, combined with 40 hours of professional training relevant to banking operations or payment services, followed under the conditions in point 2° of paragraph I, during the same three years;
2. cumulative evidence of:
   (a) achieving the competence level required under Article R. 519-9 (as follows in the next paragraph for exclusive agent) and having at least one year of professional experience in functions related to banking operations or payment services in one of the categories mentioned in paragraph I of this article;
   (b) a 40-hour professional training programme adapted to banking operations or payment services, followed under the conditions in point 2° of paragraph I, during the three years prior to registration in the unified register referred to in Article L. 546-1.

Requirements for the exclusive agent in banking operations and payment services (R. 519-4-1-2°) and for their representatives (Agent of an intermediary in banking operations and payment services according to R. 519-4-1-4°)[23]

IOBSP mentioned under point 2° of paragraph I of Article R. 519-4 and their representatives under point 4° of the same paragraph, as well as representatives of intermediaries referred to in point 1° of the same paragraph when they perform intermediation activities beyond providing a product or service, must provide evidence of professional competence demonstrated through:

1. a diploma certifying a first cycle of higher education corresponding to level 5 of the national qualifications framework;
2. 80 hours of professional training relevant to banking operations or payment services, completed with:

[23] Article R519-9

(a) a credit institution, financial company, payment institution, e-money institution providing payment services, insurance company or intermediary in banking operations and payment services as defined in Articles R. 519-8 and R. 519-9, different from the entity where such intermediaries operate;
(b) a training organisation chosen by the individual, their employer or, if applicable, their principal, under the conditions specified in Article R. 519-12.

By way of derogation, intermediaries are considered to have professional competence when they can demonstrate:

1. One year of professional experience in functions related to banking operations or payment services acquired within three years prior to registration in the unified register referred to in Article L. 546-1, combined with 40 hours of professional training relevant to banking operations or payment services, followed under the conditions specified in point 2° of paragraph I;
2. Cumulative evidence of:
   (a) achieving the competence level required under Article R. 519-10 and having at least one year of professional experience in functions related to banking operations or payment services;
   (b) a 40-hour professional training programme relevant to banking operations or payment services, followed under the conditions specified in point 2° of paragraph I, during the three years prior to registration in the unified register referred to in Article L. 546-1.

Requirements for the exclusive agent in banking operations and payment services (R. 519-4-1-2°), non-exclusive agent (R. 519-4-1-3°), and for their representatives (Agent of an intermediary in banking operations and payment services according to R. 519-4-1-4°). This article only applies to intermediaries acting in an ancillary capacity[24]

IOBSP mentioned under point 2° and 3° of paragraph I of Article R. 519-4, and their agents under point 4° of the same paragraph, must provide evidence of professional competence demonstrated through (Article R519-10):

1. a diploma certifying a first cycle of higher education at level 5 of the national qualifications framework;

---

[24] Article R519-10

2. six months of professional experience in functions related to banking operations or payment services acquired in the two years prior to registration in the unified register referred to in Article L. 546-1;
3. or sufficient professional training relevant to banking operations and payment services, completed:
    (a) with a credit institution, financial company, payment institution, e-money institution providing payment services or insurance company;
    (b) at a training organisation chosen by the individual, their employer or, if applicable, their principal, under conditions specified by the Minister of Economy.

By way of derogation, intermediaries involved in intermediation related to credits referred to in Article L. 313-1 of the Consumer Code meet the professional competence requirements of Article L. 314-24 of the same code, under the conditions set out in Articles
    D. 314-23, D. 314-24 and D. 314-26 of the same code.

The diploma referred to in the first paragraphs of Articles R. 519-8, R. 519-9 and R. 519-10 must attest to training in at least one of the following subjects: finance, banking, management, economics, law, or insurance (Article R. 519-11).

Membership and Operations of Professional Associations for Banking and Payment Service Intermediaries in France[25]

According to the French law, it is required for IOBSP to be registered in the register mentioned in Article L. 546-1, which outlines the registration requirements for intermediaries involved in banking operations, payment services, financial investment advice, tied agents and crowdfunding intermediaries. For the purposes of their registration in the register mentioned before, brokers and their agents, along with their representatives, must join an authorised professional association (the professional association is a non-profit association with a registered office in France) responsible for monitoring their activities and supporting its members[26]. This representative professional association provides mediation services, verifies the conditions for accessing and conducting their activities, ensures compliance with professional and organisational requirements and offers support and observation of activities and professional practices, particularly through the collection of statistical data.

---

[25] Only applies to brokers and their agents. Agents of credit or financial institutions are not in the scope of this obligation of joining a professional obligation.

[26] Article L519-11

The professional associations referred are approved by the ACPR, which assesses their representativeness, the competence and integrity of their legal representatives and administrators, the impartiality of their governance (evaluated based on their written procedures), and their ability to carry out and sustain their missions through adequate material and human resources[27].

Laws and Relevant Authorities in France

The French regulatory framework governing intermediaries in the banking and payment services sector provides ("IOBSP") a regulatory environment designed to safeguard consumer interests, maintain market integrity and ensure the stability of the financial system. The *Organisme pour le Registre des Intermédiaires en Assurance et Banque* (ORIAS) oversees the registration of intermediaries.

In France, the distinction is made between:

- brokers, who are under the direct control of the ACPR (the supervisory authority). They must belong to an approved professional association, which guarantees their compliance with the rules,
- agents, considered as essential outsourced service providers, who are under the control of their principals, credit institutions or financing companies (internal control).

The **French Monetary and Financial Code** (*Code Monétaire et Financier*) serves as the code of financial and banking regulation in France. It encompasses provisions to govern the activities of financial institutions, service providers and intermediaries. Within Part V, Title I, Chapter IX, dedicated attention is given to IOBSP, specifically addressing their roles, responsibilities and oversight mechanisms. One notable focus in the Regulatory Section (*Partie réglementaire*) is the framework established under Section 4 – Missions of Approved Professional Associations, with a particular emphasis on Subsection 1 – Mediation.

Another regulatory reference relevant to credit intermediaries is the **French Consumer Code** (*Code de la Consommation*). This legislation establishes specific rules governing consumer credit, which are directly applicable to intermediaries facilitating such credit arrangements. These

---

[27] Article L519-13

provisions aim to ensure transparency, fairness and consumer protection throughout the credit process.

The Consumer Code imposes obligations on intermediaries to provide clear and accurate information to clients and avoid misleading practices. Additionally, it outlines specific requirements for pre-contractual information, including disclosures about the terms, costs and risks of credit agreements. These rules complement the provisions in the French Monetary and Financial Code, forming a legal framework that regulates the activities of intermediaries.

The French Consumer Code (*Code de la Consommation*)[28] provides the legal framework governing consumer protection, even within credit operations and intermediaries. It aims to protect borrowers while ensuring the integrity and transparency of credit-related activities. Title I of the Code focuses on defining terms and regulating credit operations, including consumer credit, advertising and contractual obligations. It establishes guidelines for lenders and credit intermediaries, specifying their roles, responsibilities and the conditions under which they may operate. Central to this framework is the protection of consumers from unfair practices and excessive financial obligations. This is achieved through mandatory disclosures, clear advertising standards and detailed pre-contractual information requirements. For instance, intermediaries must provide borrowers with the necessary documentation to compare offers and assess their financial commitments. Moreover, the Code prohibits misleading advertisements and outlines sanctions for non-compliant behaviours. The legislation also includes specific provisions on the evaluation of borrower solvency, requiring lenders to perform thorough assessments before granting credit. The inclusion of solvency checks highlights the emphasis on responsible lending and the prevention of over-indebtedness. Additionally, advertising regulations ensure transparency, mandating the disclosure of main credit information, such as annual percentage rates (APRs) and total costs.

---

[28] All provisions are subject to modifications with the transposition of the CCD.

Open Access This chapter is licensed under the terms of the Creative Commons Attribution 4.0 International License (http://creativecommons.org/licenses/by/4.0/), which permits use, sharing, adaptation, distribution and reproduction in any medium or format, as long as you give appropriate credit to the original author(s) and the source, provide a link to the Creative Commons license and indicate if changes were made.

The images or other third party material in this chapter are included in the chapter's Creative Commons license, unless indicated otherwise in a credit line to the material. If material is not included in the chapter's Creative Commons license and your intended use is not permitted by statutory regulation or exceeds the permitted use, you will need to obtain permission directly from the copyright holder.

CHAPTER 4

Germany

Abstract This chapter analyzes the German system of credit intermediation, focusing on the legal framework, licensing requirements, and supervisory structures. In Germany, credit intermediaries are supervised by Trade Supervisory Authorities at the federal state level (Bundesländer). The chapter outlines the obligations of intermediaries operating in the German credit market, including competence, transparency, and other criteria. It highlights Germany's approach to licensing, which distinguishes between consumer and mortgage credit intermediation.

Keywords Germany • Bundesländer • Trade Supervisory Authorities • credit brokers • mortgage credit • consumer credit • regulatory framework

In Germany, the regulatory architecture is anchored in the Gewerbeordnung (GewO) with supervision devolved to the Trade Supervisory Authorities of the federal state level (Bundesländer). Credit intermediaries in Germany are subject to numerous requirements (civil law, trade, commerce and industry law). Furthermore, credit intermediaries are subject to the German Brokers' and Commercial Developers' Ordinance (Makler- und

© The Author(s) 2026
U. Filotto et al. (eds.), *The European Framework of Credit Intermediaries*
https://doi.org/10.1007/978-3-032-05942-0_4

Bauträgerverordnung (MaBV)). According to the German Civil Code and the Introductory Act to the German Civil Code, credit intermediaries have to comply with a specific set of disclosure rules and regulations, especially in the context of consumer credit.

CREDIT INTERMEDIARIES IN GERMANY

The term "credit intermediary" is not legally defined in Germany [in Germany, there is only a regulation with regard to the "credit mediation contract" (German Civil Act = Bürgerliches Gesetzbuch, BGB: Section 655a and the following)]. But according to German law, a credit intermediary is an individual or a firm that does not directly provide credit itself but rather facilitates an individual or a firm obtaining access to such credit from a third-party credit provider (in Germany, typically a bank). This includes intermediaries tied to one or more particular credit providers and those that are fully independent. Credit intermediaries are: financial agents, credit brokers and dealers/retailers at the point-of-sale. The end borrower might be a consumer or a business.

Section 655a and the following of the German Civil Code (BGB) focus on the rules and obligations surrounding the intermediation of consumer credit contracts and paid financial assistance provided by credit intermediaries. It outlines how contracts should be structured, the responsibilities of intermediaries, and the conditions for remuneration.

The section § 655a defines a credit intermediation contract as an agreement where a business (the intermediary) assists a consumer in:

1. entering into a consumer loan agreement or arranging paid financial assistance.
2. Finding opportunities to enter into such agreements.
3. Providing other support for the conclusion of such agreements.

This regulatory requirement ensures that only qualified and reputable individuals or firms can act as credit intermediaries. Under Section 34c[1] of the Trade, Commerce and Industry Regulation Act (Gewerbeordnung, GewO), credit intermediaries operating in the mortgage credit market need a special license under Section 34i GewO in conjunction with the German Mortgage Credit Mediation Ordinance (*Verordnung über Immobiliardarlehensvermittlung*). An exception to this requirement is

---

[1] https://www.gesetze-im-internet.de/gewo/__34c.html

made for retailers and dealers at the point of sale, who are not subjected to the same stringent licensing criteria.

The section § 655c regarding remuneration for Intermediary Services outlines that the consumer is only required to pay a commission to the credit intermediary if:

- the loan is actually granted to the consumer as a result of the intermediary's services.
- The consumer does not exercise their right of withdrawal (as outlined in § 355, which covers the right to revoke certain contracts within a specific period).

For cases where the consumer uses the loan arranged through the intermediary to refinance an existing loan (renegotiation), the intermediary is only entitled to a commission if the nominal annual interest rate does not increase as a result of the refinancing. Additionally, any intermediary fees from the previous loan are not considered when calculating the annual rate of the refinanced loan.

The law (Section § 655d related to Additional Costs) restricts intermediaries from charging any fees beyond the agreed remuneration (per § 655c) and any agreed fees for advisory services. However, it allows for repayment of actual expenses incurred by the intermediary while providing their services. This repayment is capped at amounts that the intermediary must disclose to the consumer in advance, ensuring transparency.

Credit Intermediary and Licensing Requirements for Credit Intermediaries

In Germany, credit intermediaries (financial agents and credit brokers; exception for retailers/dealers at point-of-sale) are subject to a licensing requirement under Section 34c of the Trade, Commerce and Industry Regulation Act (*Gewerbeordnung, GewO*). Credit intermediaries operating in the mortgage credit market need a special license under Section 34i GewO in conjunction with the German Mortgage Credit Mediation Ordinance (*Verordnung über Immobiliardarlehensvermittlung*).

The key criteria for applying to be licensed as a credit intermediary are set out in Section 34c and Section 34i GewO. Section 34i GewO is complemented by the Mortgage Credit Mediation Ordinance (*Verordnung über Immobiliardarlehensvermittlung*), which includes more detailed professional (entry and ongoing) requirements. In essence, the following needs to be provided when applying for a credit mediation license:

- evidence of the trustworthiness and of the good repute;
- adequate financial resources;
- evidence of appropriate knowledge and competence with regard to credit products and services (this means minimum standards/qualifications needed to begin acting as an intermediary); credit intermediaries operating in the mortgage credit market have to provide a certificate of competence, in order to obtain the administrative license for their services;
- credit intermediaries operating in the mortgage credit market have to register in the brokerage register before starting business.

License will be denied in the following cases:

- a criminal conviction of the applicant in the last five years
- existing debts/insolvency procedures
- if the authority has doubts about credibility or sees an imminent risk for public security.

LAWS AND RELEVANT AUTHORITIES IN GERMANY

The supervision of credit intermediaries in Germany is not conducted by the German Banking Supervisory Authority[2] (BaFin). Instead, the Trade Supervisory Authorities of the federal states (*Bundesländer*) are responsible for overseeing credit intermediaries, including financial agents and credit brokers. This decentralised approach ensures that each federal state can enforce regulations and monitor compliance effectively. This supervisory framework also applies to online loan comparison platforms or loan brokerage platforms that arrange bank loans through intermediary websites.

The main laws and regulations governing credit distribution activities in Germany are:

- Trade, Commerce and Industry Regulation Act[3] (*Gewerbeordnung*, GewO): This act outlines the regulatory framework for commercial

[2] https://www.bafin.de/EN/Homepage/homepage_node.html
[3] https://www.gesetze-im-internet.de/gewo/

activities, including the licensing requirements and conduct standards for credit intermediaries.
- Mortgage Credit Mediation Ordinance[4] (*Verordnung über Immobiliardarlehensvermittlung*): This ordinance specifies detailed professional requirements for mortgage credit intermediaries, covering education, training and professional conduct.
- Brokers' and Commercial Developers' Ordinance[5] (Makler- und Bauträgerverordnung, MaBV): This ordinance includes comprehensive professional standards for brokers, particularly concerning accounting practices and duties of information and disclosure.
- German Civil Code[6] (*Bürgerliches Gesetzbuch*, BGB): The BGB provides the legal foundation for various aspects of credit mediation, including contractual obligations and consumer protection.
- Introductory Act to the German Civil Code[7] (*Einführungsgesetz zum Bürgerlichen Gesetzbuch*, EGBGB): This act includes additional provisions related to the implementation and interpretation of the BGB, particularly in the context of consumer credit.

---

[4] https://www.gesetze-im-internet.de/immvermv/
[5] https://www.gesetze-im-internet.de/gewo_34cdv/index.html
[6] https://www.gesetze-im-internet.de/bgb/
[7] https://www.gesetze-im-internet.de/bgbeg/

Open Access This chapter is licensed under the terms of the Creative Commons Attribution 4.0 International License (http://creativecommons.org/licenses/by/4.0/), which permits use, sharing, adaptation, distribution and reproduction in any medium or format, as long as you give appropriate credit to the original author(s) and the source, provide a link to the Creative Commons license and indicate if changes were made.

The images or other third party material in this chapter are included in the chapter's Creative Commons license, unless indicated otherwise in a credit line to the material. If material is not included in the chapter's Creative Commons license and your intended use is not permitted by statutory regulation or exceeds the permitted use, you will need to obtain permission directly from the copyright holder.

CHAPTER 5

Italy

Abstract This chapter presents the regulatory and institutional framework for credit intermediaries in Italy, with a particular focus on the role of the Organismo per la gestione degli Elenchi degli Agenti in attività finanziaria e dei Mediatori creditizi (OAM). It explores the distinction between agents and brokers, licensing procedures, and professional standards required by law. The chapter emphasizes Italy's strong regulatory framework, including requirements and continuous professional training obligations. It also highlights Italy's national specificities in consumer protection, transparency, and the clear separation between agents and brokers.

Keywords Italy • OAM • agents • brokers • licensing • transparency • consumer protection • EU regulation

Italy maintains a centralised and structured regulatory system for credit intermediaries, managed under the supervision of the OAM, a delegated authority under the Bank of Italy's oversight. Legislative Decree No. 141/2010 lays out the regulatory framework, creating distinct categories for agents in financial activity and credit brokers, each with specific requirements regarding registration, compliance and training. This chapter outlines the legal distinctions, the authorisation procedures and the broader context of credit access policies in Italy.

© The Author(s) 2026
U. Filotto et al. (eds.), *The European Framework of Credit Intermediaries*
https://doi.org/10.1007/978-3-032-05942-0_5

Credit Intermediaries in Italy

Legislative Decree No. 141/2010, introduced on 13 August 2010, restructured the regulation of financial agents and credit brokers in Italy, and it strengthened consumer protection, professional requirements and oversight mechanisms. The decree mandates integrity, financial stability and technical-IT standards, along with enhanced internal controls and external supervision.

A key outcome was the creation of the OAM, responsible for managing professional lists and registers[1]. The OAM oversees, among other activities, compliance standards and ensures the honourability and competence of registered professionals.

The decree distinguishes between financial agents, who operate on behalf of financial institutions, and credit brokers, who act as intermediaries without ties to specific lenders.

In the next section, details on these aspects are provided.

Agents

In Title IV of the decree, the definition of agent in financial activity is provided: *"an agent in financial activity is the person who promotes and concludes contracts relating to the granting of financing in any form, on the direct mandate of financial intermediaries envisaged by Title V, institutions of payment, electronic money institutions, banks or the Italian Post. Agents in financial activity can exclusively carry out the activity indicated in this paragraph, as well as related or instrumental activities."*[2]

The agent's main activity is therefore to promote the product of its principal and conclude the relevant contract, or the granting of financing, or the provision of payment services. The promotion concerns the solicitation and development of financing contracts and payment services. The conclusion of contracts, instead, relates to the possibility of signing them in the name and on behalf of the lender.

Furthermore, *"the professional exercise of the activity of an agent in financial activity towards the public is reserved for subjects registered in a specific list kept by the OAM provided for by the Art. 128-undecies."*[3] To be able to carry out the activity of an agent, it is therefore necessary to evaluate the

---

[1] Articles 128-quater and 128-sexies of the TUB
[2] Art. 128-quater, paragraph 1, TUB
[3] Art. 128-quater, paragraph 2, TUB

requirements established by law and to register on a specific list. Carrying out the activity without registration in the list represents a crime.

The agent, as previously mentioned, operates through the institution of the mandate that can be granted to him by: financial intermediaries, payment institutions, electronic money institutions, banks and *Poste Italiane*. Its activity can be carried out on the basis of the mandate of a single intermediary or of multiple intermediaries belonging to the same group (128-quater) in order not to create conflicts of interest that could damage competition between financial intermediaries. The OAM has identified, in Circular 3/12 of 5 April 2012, the range of products and services for which a mandate can be granted to agents in financial activity:

- mortgages;
- *CQS/P*;
- factoring;
- purchase of credits;
- vehicle and aircraft leasing;
- real estate leasing;
- instrumental leasing;
- leasing on renewable sources and other types of investments;
- current account credit openings;
- personal credit;
- finalised credit;
- pawnshop loan;
- issuing sureties and guarantees;
- collective guarantee of credit lines;
- advances and commercial discounts;
- revolving credit;
- credit restructuring;
- money transfer;
- credit and debit cards;
- collection and transfer of funds and other payment services.

Furthermore, Agents in financial activity can make use of employees and collaborators to carry out their related activities towards the public[4]. The collaborator is the one who operates on the basis of an agency contract[5]: he is, in fact, regulated through the case of sub-agency. To carry out the

---

[4] Art. 128-novies of the TUB

[5] Art. 1742 c.c., Art. 17 d.lgs. n. 141/2010

activity in support of the agent, the agent must have passed an assessment test and the agent must have sent their name to the OAM. Collaborators must meet the requirements of good repute and professionalism. In particular, for the second requirement, they must:

1. possess a qualification not lower than an upper secondary education diploma;
2. attend a professional training course in the subjects relevant to carrying out the activity.

They do not have to pass the exam, but are, however, required to pass an evaluation test whose contents are established in the OAM Circular no. 5/12[6]. The TUB[7] provides for the obligation to register in the list kept by the OAM for employees and collaborators (who are employed in front office/relationship roles) of agents in financial activities who operate as natural persons or as partnerships. Otherwise, agents established in the form of joint-stock companies or cooperative companies can make use of employees and collaborators without the qualification of agents registered in the list. It is envisaged that the collaborators of agents in financial activity are exclusively natural persons who cannot simultaneously carry out their activities in favour of more than one registered entity[8] to avoid the loss of responsibilities borne by the bank or the principal financial intermediary, as well as conflicts of interest. There are various obligations

---

[6] The Proficiency Test provided for by Art. 128-novies, paragraph 1, of the TUB consists in passing a test to verify the preparation acquired at the end of a training course relating to the subjects relevant to agency activities in financial activities and credit mediation.

Members must verify that each of their employees and collaborators pursuant to Art. 128-novies of the TUB have passed the Proficiency Test and obtained the certificate. The training course, which may consist of classroom or distance learning courses, must have a total duration of no less than 20 hours, of which at least 8 hours must be carried out in the classroom or with equivalent methods. The methods of delivery of the courses via videoconferencing or e-learning methods with the provision of audiovisual tools to the learners and with the indication of the days and times in which the lessons are simultaneously used by those enrolled in the course are considered equivalent. The use of the course must be tracked and the learners must have the possibility, in the period indicated for the course, to contact the teacher who appears on video by telephone to request clarifications and clarifications. The distance courses, where provided, must precede the activity carried out in the classroom or with the equivalent methods indicated in the previous paragraph and must be designed and implemented by the same body that provides the part of the courses used in the classroom.

[7] Art. 128-novies

[8] Art. 128-octies TUB

borne by agents in financial activity regarding employees and collaborators. They must verify that they comply with the rules that govern them, that they possess the requirements of good repute and professionalism, and that they carry out the required professional updating. Furthermore, they must communicate to the OAM within ten days of the change any update relating to the list of employees and collaborators they use[9]. As regards the incompatibilities of employees and collaborators, it is expected that they cannot carry out credit mediation activities, nor carry out, even through third parties, administration, management or control activities in the credit brokerage companies registered in the list referred to in the article 128-sexies of the TUB, paragraph 2, or, even informally, promotional activities on behalf of financial intermediaries other than the one for which they provide their activity.

Brokers

Title IV of the decree provides the definition of credit broker: "*a credit broker is the person who brings together, also through consultancy activities, banks or financial intermediaries envisaged by Title V with potential customers for the granting of financing in any form.*"[10] Legislative Decree No. 141/2010 also established that, regardless of the corporate form chosen, the minimum capital required is 50,000 euros, equal to that for the establishment of public companies. The mediator, in carrying out his activity, has the task of:

1. identify the customer's financial needs;
2. translate your financial needs into the most appropriate form of financing;
3. describe and evaluate the characteristics of the financial services offered on the market.

The mediation activity can take the form of advice, in the investigation of loan applications, in the forwarding of credit requests to the financial

---

[9] The ministerial decree n. 31 of 2014 of the Ministry of Economy and Finance, in specifying the organisational requirements that credit brokers must have in implementation of Legislative Decree No. 141 of 2010, clarifies that for employees and collaborators:
- credit brokerage companies apply rigorous selection procedures for their employees and collaborators, acquiring and preserving the evidentiary documentation of the requirements possessed.

[10] Art. 128-sexies

intermediary: "*The professional exercise of the activity is reserved for subjects registered in a specific list kept by the OAM.*"[11]

For the exercise of their activities towards the public, credit brokers may make use of employees and collaborators[12]. The regulations on employees and collaborators refer exclusively to subjects who come into contact with the public on behalf of the credit intermediary. As for the collaborators of agents in financial activities, also in this case, the passing of an assessment test is required and the subsequent transmission, by the credit brokerage company, of the name of the collaborator to the OAM. Credit brokers periodically transmit the list of their employees and collaborators[13] to the Body, promptly communicating (within ten days) any changes. According to the provisions of the TUB[14], the collaborators of credit brokers can only be natural persons and cannot carry out «simultaneously their activity in favour of more than one registered person» in order to maintain the close relationship between the collaborator and the person for whom he/she works by clearly recognizing the joint and several liability of the mediator for the damage caused by the collaborator, and by avoiding a long distribution chain which entails an excessive cost by the final consumer.

As with agents, credit brokers are responsible for ensuring and verifying that their employees and collaborators comply with the regulations, possess the requirements of good repute and professionalism (excluding passing the exam) and provide professional updating. These obligations protect the customers of credit brokers, as they are jointly and severally liable for damages caused in carrying out their business by the employees and collaborators they employ.

CREDIT INTERMEDIARY AND LICENSING REQUIREMENTS FOR CREDIT INTERMEDIARIES

Legislative Decree No. 141/2010 establishes licensing requirements for financial agents and credit brokers in the OAM Register, and it ensures high professional standards in credit intermediation.

---

[11] Art. 128-sexies TUB
[12] See Art. 128-novies of the TUB
[13] Art. 128-novies TUB
[14] Art. 128-octies

To qualify for registration, applicants must meet specific requirements of professionalism, integrity and financial solidity. This includes passing competency exams, demonstrating honourability (absence of criminal records or financial misconduct) and fulfilling technical and IT prerequisites to ensure compliance with industry regulations. Additionally, ongoing training obligations are imposed to maintain and update professional skills.

The OAM is responsible for evaluating registration applications, periodic compliance checks and potential removals from the register in case of non-compliance. These measures aim to strengthen transparency, consumer protection and trust in the financial intermediation sector.

In the next section, more details on these aspects are provided.

Agents

For the purposes of registration in the list, agents in financial activities are required[15] to have:

1. for natural person agents:
   (a) to Italian citizenship or citizenship of a European Union state;
   (b) domicile in Italy;
   (c) possession of the requirements of good repute[16];
   (d) educational qualification not lower than a high school diploma;
2. for legal person agents:
   (a) registered and administrative headquarters or, for EU entities, permanent establishment in the territory of the Republic;
   (b) requirements of good repute and professionalism, including passing a specific exam;
   (c) a civil liability insurance policy for damages caused in the exercise of the activity resulting from their own conduct or that of third parties for whose actions they are liable in accordance with the law.

Remaining on the list is subject, in addition to the requirements indicated, to the effective exercise of the activity and professional updating. In particular, the requirements to be maintained are required of members and reported in the articles. 128-quinquies and 128-septies of the TUB are:

---

[15] Art. 128-quinquies TUB
[16] Art. 15 of Legislative Decree No. 141/2010

1. the professionalism requirement: provides that members must possess a qualification no lower than a five-year upper secondary education diploma, attend professional refresher courses in matters relating to the activity of an agent in financial activity and pass a specific examination called by the OAM (articles 14 and 24 of the decree).
A specification must be made for individuals with administrative, management and control functions who, in addition to the criteria already listed, must have gained overall experience of at least three years through the exercise of:
   (a) administration or control activities in enterprises;
   (b) professional activities in matters relating to the credit, financial or securities sector;
   (c) activities in university education in legal or economic subjects;
   (d) management positions in public institutions in the credit, financial or securities sector.

   The Chairman of the Board of Directors, the sole Director, the sole shareholder of the limited company and the General Manager are required to have enhanced experience in positions of appropriate responsibility in companies in the financial sector-insurance for at least five years;
2. the requirement of good repute: it does not consist in having specific qualifications but rather in the absence of situations which could compromise the moral integrity of the person. It provides that those who:
   (a) they are in one of the conditions of ineligibility or revocation provided for by Art. 2382 c.c[17];
   (b) have been subjected to preventive measures ordered by the judicial authority;
   (c) have been sentenced by an irrevocable sentence, without prejudice to the effects of rehabilitation, to imprisonment exceeding a certain threshold[18];

---

[17] An interdict, an incapacitated person, a bankrupt person or anyone who has been sentenced to a sentence which involves disqualification, even temporary, from holding public offices or the inability to exercise management offices.

[18] The prison sentence must follow: one of the crimes provided for by the rules governing financial activity, one of the crimes provided for in Title XI of Book V of the Civil Code. and by bankruptcy law, for a crime against the public administration, for any non-negligent crime resulting in imprisonment for a period of not less than two years.

3. the capital requirement: requires members to take out a civil liability insurance policy[19] for damage caused in the exercise of the activity by their own conduct or that of third parties for whose actions the agents are liable[20];
4. the technical-IT requirement includes the obligation to have a certified email inbox and a digital signature[21].

The requirements to remain on the list concern:

1. actual exercise of the activity[22];
2. professional updating in order to maintain an appropriate level of professionalism;
3. payment of annual contributions for registration in the list[23].

Brokers

For the purposes of registration in the lists, credit brokers are required to have[24]:

1. form of public company, limited liability company, limited liability company or cooperative company;
2. registered and administrative headquarters or, for EU entities, permanent establishment in the territory of the Republic;
3. corporate purpose compliant with the provisions of Article 128-sexies, paragraph 3 and compliance with the organisational requirements;
4. possession of the requirements of good repute by those in control and by the subjects who carry out administration, management and control functions;

---

[19] The policy limits are commensurate with the volume of activity of the agent and are established by the OAM with Circular 1/12. After stipulation, the details of the policy must be communicated to the OAM on the date of registration in the list (Art. 23, Legislative Decree No. 141/2010). Until such data is communicated, the agent will be registered as "non-operational," a situation which cannot exceed one year as this would then be one of the causes that would lead to cancellation from the list.

[20] Art. 16 of the decree

[21] Art. 18 of the decree

[22] Inactivity lasting more than a year leads to cancellation from the list (Art. 128-duodiecies, paragraph 3).

[23] The quotas are established by the OAM also based on the number of employees and collaborators in the case of a legal entity.

[24] Art. 128-septies TUB

5. possession by the subjects who carry out administrative, management and control functions of professionalism requirements, including passing a specific exam;
6. a civil liability insurance policy for damages caused in the exercise of activities resulting from their own conduct or that of third parties for whose actions they are liable in accordance with the law.

Further requirements required of credit brokers provided for by the decree are:

1. *Professionalism requirement*. It provides that individuals with administrative and management functions must have gained at least three years' experience through the exercise of one of the following activities:

(a) administration or control activities at companies;
(b) professional activities on matters relating to the credit, financial or securities sector;
(c) university teaching activities in legal or economic subjects;
(d) managerial roles in public bodies relating to the credit, financial or securities sector.

The President of the Board of Directors, the Sole Director, the sole shareholder of the limited liability company and the General Manager are required to have at least five years' experience in the activities listed above.

Those who carry out management and administrative functions must also possess:

1. educational qualification not lower than a high school diploma;
2. attendance of a professional training course in subjects relevant to the practice of credit mediation;
3. passing a specific exam set by the Body.

2. *Honourability requirement*: does not consist in the possession of specific qualifications but rather in the absence of situations that could compromise the moral integrity of the person. It provides that those who:

(a) are in one of the conditions of ineligibility or forfeiture provided for by the Art. 2382 c.c.[25];

---

[25] An interdict, an incapacitated person, a bankrupt person, or anyone who has been sentenced to a sentence which involves disqualification, even temporary, from holding public offices or the inability to exercise management offices.

(b) have been subjected to prevention measures ordered by the judicial authority;
(c) were sentenced with an irrevocable sentence, without prejudice to the effects of rehabilitation, to a prison sentence exceeding the established threshold[26].

The requirement of good repute must also be met by those who control the credit brokerage company requesting registration on the list. If control is held by a legal person, it must be held by those who carry out administration, management and control functions thereof.

3. *Capital requirement*: credit brokerage companies are required to be set up as joint-stock companies with a minimum capital of 50,000 euros[27] in order to further guarantee the consumer against damages caused by the incorrect behaviour of employees and collaborators. Members are also required to take out a policy of insurance[28] of civil liability for damages caused in the exercise of the activity by one's own conduct or that of third parties for whose actions the mediators are responsible[29].

4. *Technical-IT requirement*: provides for the obligation to have a certified email inbox and a digital signature[30].

Finally, the requirements to remain on the list concern:

---

[26] The prison sentence must follow: one of the crimes provided for by the rules governing financial activity, one of the crimes provided for in Title XI of Book V of the Civil Code. and by bankruptcy law, for a crime against the public administration, for any non-negligent crime resulting in imprisonment for a period of not less than two years.

[27] Art. 128-septies TUB

[28] The policy limits are commensurate with the volume of activity of the agent and are established by the OAM with Circular no. 1/12. After stipulation, the details of the policy must be communicated to the OAM on the date of registration in the list (Art. 23 of Legislative Decree No. 141/2010). Until such data are communicated, the mediator will be registered as "non-operational," a situation which cannot exceed one year as this would then be one of the causes that would lead to upon deletion from the list.

[29] Art. 16 of the decree

[30] Art. 18 of the decree

(a) to the effective exercise of the activity[31];
(b) professional updating in order to maintain an appropriate level of professionalism;
(c) payment of annual contributions for registration in the list[32].

Laws and Relevant Authorities in Italy

The legislation that regulates the figure of the agent in financial activity and the credit broker is the Legislative Decree No. 141/2010, introduced on 13 August 2010. The decree, through detailed and selective rules, ensures greater protection for consumers, and it requires operators to satisfy professionalism, integrity, financial soundness, technical-IT requirements, and to strengthen the internal control system, also undergoing external checks (in particular by the OAM).

The fourth Title of the decree in question is dedicated to the revision of the regulations concerning the distribution of credit through financial agents and credit brokers.

A primary step following the entry into force of Legislative Decree No. 141/2010 was the establishment of the Body of OAM, exclusively and autonomously competent for the management of the Lists referred to in the Articles 128-quater and 128-sexies of the TUB, and holder of a series of other functions conferred on him by law such as that of evaluating the conditions for registration and cancellation from the Lists and Registers, that of ensuring the protection of consumers, guaranteeing the permanence of the professional and honourability requirements ascertained during registration.

---

[31] Inactivity lasting more than a year leads to cancellation from the list (Art. 128-duodiecies, paragraph 3, TUB).

[32] The OAM also determines the fees on the basis of the number of employees and collaborators in the case of a legal entity. It is therefore made up of a fixed share and a variable share based on the number of employees and collaborators.

Open Access This chapter is licensed under the terms of the Creative Commons Attribution 4.0 International License (http://creativecommons.org/licenses/by/4.0/), which permits use, sharing, adaptation, distribution and reproduction in any medium or format, as long as you give appropriate credit to the original author(s) and the source, provide a link to the Creative Commons license and indicate if changes were made.

The images or other third party material in this chapter are included in the chapter's Creative Commons license, unless indicated otherwise in a credit line to the material. If material is not included in the chapter's Creative Commons license and your intended use is not permitted by statutory regulation or exceeds the permitted use, you will need to obtain permission directly from the copyright holder.

CHAPTER 6

Portugal

Abstract This chapter investigates the Portuguese system of credit intermediation and the role of the Bank of Portugal. It outlines the legal and regulatory framework for credit brokers and agents, as well as the licensing procedures required to operate in mortgage and consumer credit markets. The chapter examines the supervisory role of national authorities and transparency standards.

Keywords Portugal • Bank of Portugal • credit intermediaries • mortgage credit • consumer credit • supervision

In Portugal, credit intermediation is defined and regulated by national Law, under the supervision of the Bank of Portugal. This chapter presents an overview of the legislative framework, the registration and supervision mechanisms, and the disclosure obligations toward consumers. It also reflects on the operational challenges faced by credit brokers in adapting to national and EU-level regulatory evolution.

© The Author(s) 2026
U. Filotto et al. (eds.), *The European Framework of Credit Intermediaries*
https://doi.org/10.1007/978-3-032-05942-0_6

CREDIT INTERMEDIARIES IN PORTUGAL

In Portugal, the *Decree-Law No. 81-C/2017* regulates both consumer credit and mortgage credit intermediaries. Credit intermediaries are categorised into three main types: ancillary intermediaries, untied intermediaries, and tied intermediaries, each governed by distinct legal requirements and regulatory oversight from the Bank of Portugal.

In general, a **Credit Intermediary** is a natural or legal person who, not acting as a creditor, provides services in the presentation, proposal, or conclusion of credit agreements[1] on behalf of consumers for a fee (Article 3, definition of Credit Intermediary). In the course of their activities, credit intermediaries may provide one or more of the following credit intermediation services[2]:

1. presenting or proposing credit agreements to consumers.
2. Assisting consumers by performing preparatory actions or other pre-contractual management activities related to credit agreements that they have not directly presented or proposed.
3. Concluding credit agreements with consumers on behalf of credit institutions.

In particular, Decree-Law No. 81-C/2017 defines credit intermediaries as follows:

1. Ancillary Credit Intermediary: a provider of goods or services acting on behalf of and under the full responsibility of the creditor or group with whom they have a binding contract, to promote the sale of goods or services.
2. Untied Credit Intermediary: a legal entity acting as a credit intermediary without a binding contract with a creditor or group of creditors.
3. Tied Credit Intermediary: an individual or legal entity operating as a credit intermediary under a binding contract, acting on behalf of and under the full responsibility of the creditor or group with whom the contract is made.

---

[1] A credit agreement is a contract whereby a creditor grants or commits to granting consumer credit in forms such as loans, credit lines, credit cards, or similar financial arrangements, including financial leasing and long-term rentals. On the other side, an Intermediary Contract in an agreement between a consumer and an untied credit intermediary, establishing the terms and conditions of credit intermediation services (Article 3 of the Decree-Law No. 81-C/2017).

[2] Article 4 of the Decree-Law No. 81-C/2017

In addition, credit intermediaries may not carry out activities falling into more than one of the categories outlined in the legislation[3].

Credit intermediaries can also carry out advisory activities linked to credit services[4]. Advisory services related to credit agreements involve providing personalised recommendations to consumers on specific credit agreements, separate from the intermediation or provision of credit itself. These services are aimed at helping consumers make informed financial decisions based on their personal and financial circumstances[5].

The activity of a credit intermediary can only be carried out by the following entities[6]:

a) individuals and Legal Entities with a professional domicile, registered office and central administration in Portugal, who, in accordance with this legal framework, obtain authorisation to act as credit intermediaries and are registered with the Bank of Portugal for this purpose.

b) Individuals and Legal Entities with a professional domicile, registered office or central administration in another EU Member State, who are authorised to act as credit intermediaries in their home

---

[3] Article 6 of the Decree-Law No. 81-C/2017

[4] Article 4 paragraph 3 of the Decree-Law No. 81-C/2017

[5] Only authorised entities meeting the requirements under this article are permitted to provide these advisory services in Portugal. The provision of advisory services related to credit agreements can only be conducted by the following entities:

1. Individuals and Legal Entities with a professional domicile, registered office, and central administration in Portugal, who are authorised to act as credit intermediaries, registered with the Bank of Portugal, and also authorised to provide advisory services.
2. Individuals and Legal Entities with a professional domicile, registered office, or central administration in another EU Member State, who are authorised to act as credit intermediaries in their home Member State for mortgage credit agreements and are registered with the competent authority of that Member State. These entities must also be authorised by their home state's competent authority to provide advisory services related to mortgage credit agreements.
3. Credit Institutions, Financial Companies, Payment Institutions and Electronic Money Institutions that are legally authorised to operate in Portugal.

If there is reasonable suspicion that an unauthorised entity is providing or has provided advisory services, regulatory action may be taken (Article 7 of the Decree-Law No. 81-C/2017)

[6] Article 5 of the Decree-Law No. 81-C/2017

Member State for mortgage credit agreements and are registered with the competent authority of that Member State. These entities may operate in Portugal to provide services they are authorised to offer in their home Member State, in compliance with the terms and conditions established in this legal framework.

c) Credit Institutions, Financial Companies, Payment Institutions and Electronic Money Institutions that are legally authorised to operate in Portugal in relation to credit agreements in which they do not act as lenders.

Remuneration of Credit Intermediaries in Portugal

Art. 58 and Art. 61 of the Decree-Law No. 81-C/2017, together with Notice of the Bank of Portugal No. 6/2017, outline the remuneration policy.

Tied credit intermediaries and ancillary credit intermediaries can be compensated only by the lenders (i.e., the institutions granting the credit) and are prohibited from receiving any payment or other form of economic compensation from consumers, including fees, commissions or charges.

Lending institutions must ensure that the remuneration of credit intermediaries does not compromise compliance with the conduct obligations imposed on credit intermediaries, namely the duties of diligence, loyalty, discretion and conscientious respect for consumer interests.

Untied credit intermediaries are compensated solely by consumers and are prohibited from receiving any remuneration or other economic compensation from lenders for the services they provide.

Before providing such services, untied credit intermediaries must inform the consumer of the service fees and any other charges. These details must also be clearly included in the credit intermediation agreement concluded between the credit intermediary and the consumer.

According to Article 45 of the Decree-Law (*"Prohibition on receiving and delivering valuables"*), all kinds of credit intermediaries are prohibited from receiving or delivering any amounts related to the formation, execution and early fulfilment of credit agreements.

CREDIT INTERMEDIARY AND LICENSING REQUIREMENTS FOR CREDIT INTERMEDIARIES

As previously mentioned, under Portugal's Decree-Law No. 81-C/2017, credit intermediaries, including those for mortgage and consumer credit, must fulfil licensing and registration requirements. Individuals and entities intending to operate as credit intermediaries or provide advisory services in Portugal must obtain authorisation[7] from the Bank of Portugal, ensuring they meet requirements like Portuguese or EU nationality, legal capacity, recognised suitability, adequate knowledge in credit contracts and a suitable organisational structure[8].

The requirements for credit intermediaries, including those for mortgage and consumer credit intermediaries, under Portugal's *Decree-Law No. 81-C/2017* cover different criteria necessary to obtain and to maintain authorisation to operate, distinguishing between individuals and legal entities.

Authorisation for **individuals** is conditional upon meeting the following criteria:

1. **Nationality**: Individuals must be Portuguese nationals, nationals of another EU member state or from a third country that offers reciprocal treatment to Portuguese nationals;
2. **Professional Domicile**: Individuals must have a professional domicile in Portugal, ensuring their accessibility within the national territory;
3. **Age and Legal Capacity**: The applicant must be of legal age and possess the capacity to conduct commercial activities;
4. **Suitability**: Candidates must meet suitability criteria, which are defined in a subsequent article, to ensure a trustworthy character;
5. **Knowledge and Competence**: Credit intermediaries must have adequate knowledge of credit contracts, consumer rights and credit risk, validated by relevant certifications or experience, according to Article 13 of the Decree-Law No. 81-C/2017[9].

---

[7] Article 11 of the Decree-Law No. 81-C/2017

[8] Article 5 of the Decree-Law No. 81-C/2017

[9] Requirement of Knowledge and Competencies. For the purposes of this regulation, adequate knowledge and competencies are considered to involve a thorough understanding of the following areas:

1. The characteristics of credit products sold and the associated services commonly offered alongside these products.
2. The regulations applicable to credit agreements, particularly with a focus on consumer protection.
3. The process of acquiring properties when intended for individuals interested in developing credit intermediary activities related to real estate credit contracts.

6. **Commercial and Administrative Organisation**: Intermediaries are required to have a proper organisational structure, including human, technical and material resources that allow efficient and compliant operation (Article 14) (Decree-Law No. 81-C2017).
7. **Professional Liability Insurance**: Intermediaries must secure insurance to cover liabilities arising from their professional activities, ensuring compensation in case of errors or negligence (Article 15) (Decree-Law No. 81-C2017).

Authorisation for **legal entities**, whether established or to be established, depends on meeting the following conditions:

1. Must be set up as a limited liability company or joint-stock company.
2. Must have a registered office and central administration in Portugal.
3. Must have an adequate commercial and administrative organisation as per Article 14
4. Must appoint members to its administrative body who:
    (a) Meet the requirements in points (c) to (e) for individuals.
    (b) Possess adequate knowledge and competence in credit contracts as per Article 13.
    (c) Are not in situations of disqualification as defined by Article 16.
5. Must have professional liability insurance or an equivalent guarantee to cover third-party liabilities (Article 15).

4. The evaluation of guarantees typically required for credit approval.
5. The organisation and functioning of property registries when intended for individuals engaging in credit intermediary activities, or of movable goods subject to registration in other cases.
6. The credit market in Portugal.
7. The assessment of consumer creditworthiness.
8. Standards of corporate ethics.
9. Fundamental notions of economics and finance.

Individuals are considered to have adequate knowledge and competencies to carry out credit intermediary activities for private individuals if they: (a) Comply with the mandatory training requirements defined by law and hold professional certification in the field of credit intermediation, in accordance with the minimum content to be defined by the ordinance referred to in paragraph 4. Or (b) Possess an academic degree, a higher technical diploma, or a post-secondary qualification aimed at obtaining a diploma, provided the educational program includes the minimum training content defined in the ordinance referred to in paragraph 4.

(a) **Shareholding Requirements for Joint-Stock Companies**: For joint-stock companies, shares representing the company's capital must be nominative.
(b) **Employee Knowledge Requirements**: For entities providing mortgage-related credit intermediation or advisory services, employees must possess adequate knowledge and competence per Article 13.
(c) **Technical Manager Requirement**: If the intermediary does not intend to engage in mortgage credit activities or provide advisory services for mortgage-related contracts, the requirements in Article 11(2)(f) and Article 11(3)(d)(ii) are fulfilled by appointing at least one technical manager who meets the criteria in points (c) to (f) of Article 11(2) and Article 16.

Additionally, intermediaries are required to have professional liability insurance to cover potential civil liabilities arising from professional negligence. This requirement is crucial for mortgage credit intermediaries to meet EU standards, as outlined in Article 15 of the decree-law (Decree-Law No. 81-C2017). For corporate entities, only limited liability or joint-stock companies can be authorised, with obligations to maintain a commercial and administrative organisation capable of supporting credit intermediation and advisory activities (Articles 13 and 14 of Decree-Law No. 81-C2017).

Only individuals or legal entities that have entered into a binding contract with a single lender, a single group of lenders, or multiple lenders/groups that do not represent a market majority may operate as **tied** credit intermediaries[10].

For **untied** credit intermediaries, only legal entities may operate as untied credit intermediaries. Legal entities intending to operate as untied credit intermediaries must also meet the following conditions:

1. their sole corporate purpose must be the activity of credit intermediation.
2. Their capital may not include participation from:
   - Credit institutions.
   - Financial companies.
   - Payment institutions.
   - Electronic money institutions.

---

[10] Article 17 of the Decree-Law No. 81-C/2017

- Tied credit intermediaries.
- Ancillary credit intermediaries.
- Entities in which the aforementioned entities hold a stake, including related companies as defined by the Commercial Companies Code.

In general, for credit intermediaries, the authorisation granted may be revoked[11] for the following reasons, in addition to other grounds provided by law:

1. The authorisation was obtained through false or inaccurate statements or other illegal means, regardless of applicable penalties.
2. Subsequent failure to meet any of the requirements set out in Credit Intermediaries in Portugal of this chapter for access to the credit intermediary activity.
3. Serious or repeated violations of laws and regulations governing the activity of credit intermediation.
4. Failure to engage in credit intermediation activities or provide advisory services in the preceding six months.

Laws and Relevant Authorities in Portugal

Regarding the credit to consumers credit intermediation, the regime was implemented in Portugal through the Decree-Law 81-C/2017, of July 7 (hereinafter, also the "Decree-Law"), which entered into force in January 2018, with an adaptation period for those who were already acting as "credit intermediaries" up to December 2017.

In Portugal, Decree-Law No. 81-C/2017 establishes the legal framework governing the conditions for accessing the activity of a credit intermediary and providing advisory services related to credit agreements and also regulates how these activities should be performed.

The competent authority is the Bank of Portugal, to ensure compliance with access and operational requirements for credit intermediary activities and advisory services; among the requirements, there is the need to obtain authorisation to carry out the activity and registration with the Bank of Portugal itself. In particular, the Bank of Portugal is responsible for the supervision of credit intermediaries, the exercise of credit intermediary activities by credit institutions, financial companies, payment institutions

---

[11] Article 23 of the Decree-Law No. 81-C/2017

and electronic money institutions, as well as the provision of credit services and advice on credit agreements by credit intermediaries and credit institutions, financial companies, payment institutions and electronic money institutions. Specifically, the Bank of Portugal is responsible for authorising the exercise of these activities, monitoring the performance of credit intermediaries, credit institutions, financial companies, payment institutions and electronic money institutions in the exercise of the activities regulated in this Decree-Law, sanctioning any violations of the respective rules and regulating the aspects necessary for the correct implementation of the legal regime.

As outlined in Article 35 on cooperation between the Bank of Portugal and Competent Authorities of Other EU Member States, the Bank of Portugal cooperates with competent authorities in other EU Member States, particularly in information exchange and cooperation for investigation and supervision activities.

Other relevant laws in the sector are:

- Decree-Law 133/2009, also known as the Consumer Credit Legal Regime, that transposes the European Directive 2008/48/EC into Portuguese law, establishing rules for credit agreements with consumers. This legislation focuses on protecting consumers by ensuring transparency, fairness and responsible lending practices in credit transactions;
- Notice of Bank of Portugal 6/2017, published on 6 October 2017, regulates various aspects of the credit intermediary activity in Portugal, as established by Decree-Law No. 81-C/2017. This includes the authorisation process for credit intermediaries, their registration with the Bank of Portugal, and the remuneration policies for those involved in credit intermediation or providing credit-related advisory services.

Open Access This chapter is licensed under the terms of the Creative Commons Attribution 4.0 International License (http://creativecommons.org/licenses/by/4.0/), which permits use, sharing, adaptation, distribution and reproduction in any medium or format, as long as you give appropriate credit to the original author(s) and the source, provide a link to the Creative Commons license and indicate if changes were made.

The images or other third party material in this chapter are included in the chapter's Creative Commons license, unless indicated otherwise in a credit line to the material. If material is not included in the chapter's Creative Commons license and your intended use is not permitted by statutory regulation or exceeds the permitted use, you will need to obtain permission directly from the copyright holder.

CHAPTER 7

Spain

Abstract This chapter reviews the Spanish regulatory environment for credit intermediation. It discusses licensing requirements, consumer protection measures, and the supervisory responsibilities of national authorities. Consumer credit intermediaries, unlike residential immovable property credit intermediaries, are not required to register nor supervised by the Bank of Spain. Spain's framework emphasizes transparency, disclosure of commissions, and the responsibilities of intermediaries in ensuring fair treatment of consumers. The chapter also highlights challenges such as regulatory fragmentation.

Keywords Spain • Bank of Spain • credit brokers • licensing • consumer protection • transparency • financial supervision

In Spain, certain credit-related activities, such as the distribution of consumer credit or intermediation between lenders and borrowers, are not exclusively reserved for regulated financial institutions. These services can also be offered by natural or legal persons who may engage in them alongside other professional activities, including financial advisory, commercial agency or property brokerage. However, stricter regulatory requirements apply to credit intermediaries involved in residential real estate credit agreements, where specific authorisation and oversight mechanisms are in place. This chapter analyses the main regulatory provisions in the sector.

CREDIT INTERMEDIARIES IN SPAIN

In Spain, some typical activities of financial institutions, such as consumer credit intermediation between entities and consumers or the granting of credit, are not reserved for supervised institutions and can be carried out by natural or legal persons, different from financial institutions, that usually combine these activities with other activities such as advisory, agency or residential immovable property intermediation[1]. However, this does not apply to credit intermediaries providing residential immovable property credit agreements.

A consumer credit intermediary is defined by the Law 16/2011 as a natural or legal person who does not act as a lender but, in the course of their commercial or professional activity and in exchange for remuneration, which may be monetary or take any other agreed form of economic benefit, undertakes one or more of the following roles:

- presents or offers credit agreements;
- assists consumers with preliminary steps related to credit agreements, distinct from the offering or presentation of credit agreements;
- concludes credit agreements with consumers on behalf of the lender.

A consumer credit contract is an agreement whereby a lender grants or commits to granting a consumer credit in the form of deferred payment, loan, credit line or any other equivalent means of financing[2].

The following are not considered consumer credit contracts under this law: contracts for the supply of goods of the same type or for the continuous provision of services, provided the consumer retains the right to pay for such goods or services in instalments over the contract's duration.

According to this law, other parties (in addition to the credit intermediary) involved in a credit consumer contract are:

---

[1] *Banco de España* (2024) *Intermediación financiera en el mercado de crédito* [Available at: https://clientebancario.bde.es/pcb/es/menu-horizontal/productosservici/relacionados/entidades/guia-textual/tiposentidadesso/intermediacion__a7d96c8a0a53d51.html]

[2] As defined in the Art.1 of Law 16/2011

- the consumer, who is defined as a natural person who, within contractual relationships governed by this law, acts for purposes outside their commercial or professional activity.
- the lender, that is, a natural or legal person who grants or commits to granting credit in the course of their business or professional activities.

According to Article 4 of Law 5/2019, a residential immovable property credit intermediary is defined as any natural person or legal entity, other than a lender or notary public, who performs paid commercial or professional activities to facilitate loan agreements with a mortgage guarantee or other real rights of guarantee over residential property. These intermediaries can undertake the following functions:

- presenting or offering loan contracts to borrowers;
- assisting borrowers by conducting preliminary procedures or other pre-contractual management regarding loan contracts;
- entering into loan contracts with a borrower on behalf of the lender.

In addition, the Spanish legal framework also defines the figure of the Tied Credit Intermediary, who is a component of the financial intermediation, that helps and supports credit distribution. Governed by Article 4, paragraphs 7 and 8, this figure operates exclusively under the full and unconditional responsibility of a designated lender or group of lenders, maintaining a close and dependent relationship. In particular, the law defines the "Tied credit intermediary" and the "Appointed representative":

- a "tied credit intermediary" is any credit intermediary that acts on behalf of and under the full and unconditional responsibility of:
  - a single lender;
  - a single group;
  - or a number of lenders or groups that do not represent the majority of the market;
- an "appointed representative" is any natural or legal person that carries out the activities typical of a real estate credit intermediary on behalf of and under the full and unconditional responsibility of a single intermediary.

Agents

Credit institutions can be supported by the figure of the agent in carrying out their business. Agents of credit institutions are natural or legal persons authorised by a credit institution to regularly act on behalf of the institution, in the negotiation or formalisation of operations typical of credit institution activities. This does not include individuals with power of attorney for a single, specific transaction or persons employed by the institution or other entities within the same group under an employment relationship[3].

Credit institutions operating in Spain must report their list of agents to the Bank of Spain once a year in the format determined by the Bank, indicating the extent of representation granted. This list must be updated with any new representations or cancellations as they occur and included in an annexe to the institution's annual report. The Bank of Spain may request any information from both the credit institutions and their agents relevant to its areas of jurisdiction[4]. In agency contracts, credit institutions must require their agents to clearly disclose their role in all interactions with customers, unambiguously identifying the represented institution. The credit institution is responsible for ensuring compliance with regulatory and disciplinary standards in actions performed by the agent. To this end, it must implement appropriate control procedures. An agent may represent only one credit institution or credit institutions within the same consolidated credit group. Agents of credit institutions may not act through sub-agents.

Credit Intermediary and Licensing Requirements for Credit Intermediaries

In Spain, certain credit intermediation activities, such as facilitating offers or granting credit, are not restricted to regulated entities and can be performed by individuals or legal entities alongside other services that they can provide. Consumer credit intermediaries, different from residential immovable property credit intermediaries, are not required to register, nor are they supervised by the Bank of Spain.

The legal framework for real estate credit intermediaries, their representatives, and mortgage lenders, indeed, is defined by Law 5/2019. Registration is mandatory with either the Bank of Spain or the Autonomous Communities, depending on the area of operation. The Bank of Spain also

---

[3] Article 22 of Royal Decree 1245/1995
[4] Article 22, paragraph 4, of Royal Decree 1245/1995

supervises intermediaries operating through a branch or under the free provision of services regime[5].

Real estate credit intermediaries must be registered in one of the registries outlined in this law to validly engage, in whole or in part, in the credit intermediation activities described in Article 4 of Law 5/2019 or to provide advisory services[6].

Spain's Law 5/2019, of March 15, requires a prior administrative registration for residential immovable property credit lenders and intermediaries, hence recognising and establishing a specific regime for their supervision and applicable sanctions. Thus, Royal Decree 106/2011, of January 28, establishes and regulates the State Registry of companies as provided for in Law 2/2009, of March 31, and sets the minimum amount for liability insurance or bank guarantees required for the exercise of these activities. Regarding consumer protection, the management of the State Registry is done by the General Subdirectorate of Consumer Quality of the National Consumer Institute. Currently, these responsibilities are exercised by governing bodies within the Ministry of Consumption.

Registration in the appropriate registry requires prior verification by the competent authority to ensure compliance with legal and regulatory requirements. Specifically, the verification process confirms that intermediaries have[7]:

1. The required guarantee[8]
2. The technical and operational capacity to meet informational obligations[9]

---

[5] https://clientebancario.bde.es/pcb/es/menu-horizontal/productosservici/relacionados/entidades/guia-textual/tiposentidadesso/intermediacion__a7d96c8a0a53d51.html

[6] Art. 27 of the Law 5/2019

[7] Art. 29 of the Law 5/2019

[8] Article 36 of the Law 5/2019 – Guarantee requirements for real estate credit intermediaries.

Real estate credit intermediaries must have professional liability insurance or a bank guarantee to cover liabilities that may arise due to professional negligence in the territorial area in which they offer their services. Such insurance must cover, among other things, liabilities arising from failure to comply with the information obligations of borrowers. The exceptions that may correspond to the insurer against the insured credit intermediary will in no case be applicable to the borrower. However, in the case of related real estate credit intermediaries, the insurance or bank guarantee may be provided by a lender on whose behalf the credit intermediary is authorised to act. The Government shall establish by Royal Decree the minimum amount and the conditions that the professional liability insurance or bank guarantee must meet.

[9] Article 35 of the Law 5/2019

3. Intermediaries must also have appointed a representative for the Executive Service of the Commission for the Prevention of Money Laundering and Monetary Offences in compliance with Article 35.1 of the Regulation for the Prevention of Money Laundering and Terrorist Financing, approved by Royal Decree 304/2014 of May 5, provided the conditions in Article 31.1 of the Regulation are met.
4. A training plan covering the knowledge and competencies described in Article 16[10] and its implementing regulations must be maintained.

Additionally, the competent authority verifies that individuals acting as real estate credit intermediaries or administrators of intermediary legal entities meet the knowledge and competence criteria established in Article 16, possess recognised commercial and professional integrity, have no criminal record for serious offenses related to property, socio-economic order, forgery, or any other crime committed in the exercise of financial activities, and have not been declared bankrupt unless they have been rehabilitated. The competent authority also ensures compliance with other requirements established by the Government through Royal Decree. The criteria

---

[10] Article 16. Knowledge and competence requirements applicable to personnel.

1. The staff at the service of the lender, credit intermediary or designated representative must gather at all times the necessary and updated knowledge and skills regarding the products they market, and, in particular, with respect to the processing, offer or concession of loan contracts, the intermediation activity of credit, and the provision of advice services, in its case, and in the execution of the loan contracts. This obligation will also be applicable with respect to the accessory services included in the supply contracts and with respect to the products of the sales contract or combination referred to in the following article.
2. The person in charge of the Ministry of Economy and Business will establish the minimum knowledge and competence requirements required of the personnel for compliance with this article.
3. The minimum requirements for knowledge and competence established in this law and its development regulations will also be applicable to the staff of the branch of the lender or real estate credit intermediary registered in another country.

    The lender or real estate credit intermediary who acts under the regime of free provision of services must comply with the minimum requirements of knowledge and competence, which are specifically determined by the person in charge of the Ministry of Economy and Business.
4. The requirements indicated in the previous sections will be equally applicable to the persons who undertake the activity foreseen in Article 19.

for determining whether the staff of real estate credit intermediaries meet the required knowledge and competence standards under Article 16 will be published by the corresponding registries outlined in Article 27.

The competent authority managing the registry under Article 28 may revoke the authorisation to act as a real estate credit intermediary if the intermediary expressly renounces its registration or has not performed any activities or provided services as outlined in Article 4 within the six months preceding the revocation process. Revocation may also occur if the authorisation was obtained through false or misleading declarations or by other irregular means, if the intermediary no longer meets the requirements for registration, or if a final sanctioning decision imposes revocation. After hearing the intermediary, the revocation decision will result in the automatic removal of the registration from the registry. The Bank of Spain will notify the revocation to the competent authorities of the host Member States using appropriate communication means within 14 days. If the competent authority is regional, it must notify the Bank of Spain within ten days.

Laws and Relevant Authorities in Spain

As previously stated, certain activities typically associated with financial institutions, such as facilitating offers between clients and entities or granting credit, are not exclusively reserved for regulated entities. As a result, individuals or legal entities outside the scope of financial institutions can also perform these functions. Furthermore, these activities are often combined with other services, such as consultancy or real estate agency.

Since these activities do not fall under financial regulation, they are not subject to supervisory oversight by any financial authority. This means that there are no dedicated regulatory bodies monitoring in the same way as for supervised financial institutions. Consequently, participants in these sectors operate without the regulatory safeguards and oversight mechanisms that typically apply to financial intermediaries.

On the other side, the supervision of real estate credit intermediaries falls under the Bank of Spain or the competent body of the Autonomous Community, as specified in Article 28 of the Law 5/2019. The competent authority ensures that intermediaries and their representatives are registered and consistently comply with the obligations established in this law and its implementing regulations.

In Spain, the regulatory framework governing credit intermediaries is primarily defined by two pieces of legislation: Law 5/2019, of March 15, and Law 16/2011, of June 24. Law 5/2019 transposes the European Union Directive 2014/17/EU into Spanish law, specifically regulating residential immovable property credit intermediaries, including transparency, conduct rules, and mandatory registration.

In addition, credit intermediaries must comply with the obligations and other regulatory requirements imposed by consumer and users' protection regulations, under the scope of the Ministry of Consumption, and other regulatory bodies such as the Spanish Data Protection Authority. These regulations include, among others, the following:

- Law 22/2007, of July 11, on the distance marketing of financial services for consumers
- Law 10/2010, of April 28, on the prevention of money laundering or terrorist financing[11].
- Law 34/2002, of July 11, on Information Society Services and Electronic Commerce
- General Data Protection Regulation and the Organic Law 3/2018[12].

Concerning the prevention of money laundering or terrorist financing, indeed, Article 2, paragraph 1 of Law 10/2010 establishes all categories of subjects under scope and, specifically, letter k includes "people professionally dedicated to intermediation in the granting of loans or credits, as well as people who, without having obtained authorisation as financial credit establishments, professionally carry out any of the activities referred to in the first additional provision of Law 3/1994, of April 14, which adapts Spanish legislation on Credit Institutions to the Second Banking Coordination Directive and introduces other modifications related to the Financial System." Furthermore, Article 2, paragraph 2 specifies that "the obligated subjects will also be subject to the obligations established in this Law with respect to operations carried out through agents or other persons who act as mediators or intermediaries for them."

---

[11] This law focuses on the prevention of money laundering and terrorist financing. It imposes obligations on credit intermediaries and other financial entities to implement measures to prevent financial crimes, including the requirement to report suspicious transactions.

[12] These laws govern data protection and privacy in Spain, applicable to all entities handling personal data, including credit intermediaries and financial institutions. They ensure that personal data is processed lawfully, fairly and transparently.

With reference to the relevant authorities in the Spanish credit intermediation sector, the following entities are:

1. Bank of Spain (Banco de España): The central authority responsible for overseeing and regulating the activities of credit institutions and intermediaries in Spain. The Bank of Spain ensures that financial entities comply with national and EU regulations, maintains financial stability and supervises the proper conduct of banks and other credit providers.
2. Ministry of Economic Affairs and Digital Transformation (*Ministerio de Asuntos Económicos y Transformación Digital*): This ministry is responsible for setting the overall economic policy framework, including financial regulation and supervision. It formulates policies related to credit distribution and the protection of consumers within the financial sector.
3. Ministry of Consumption (*Ministerio de Consumo*): This ministry oversees consumer protection, ensuring that consumers' rights are safeguarded in various sectors; hence, non-supervised financial services players must comply with the "broader consumer protection regulatory framework." It regulates the activities of non-bank credit intermediaries and ensures they adhere to consumer protection laws.
4. Spanish Data Protection Authority (*Agencia Española de Protección de Datos, AEPD*): The AEPD is responsible for ensuring compliance with data protection laws in Spain, including the General Data Protection Regulation (GDPR). It oversees how credit intermediaries and financial institutions handle personal data, ensuring that privacy rights are respected.

In addition to the authorities previously mentioned, among the other relevant entities active in this sector, there are the following associations:

5. ASNEF (*Asociación Nacional de Establecimientos Financieros de Crédito*): ASNEF is the Spanish trade association representing regulated financial institutions that primarily provide consumer credit. It is a member of Eurofinas, the European Federation of Finance House Associations, and it advocates for the interests of regulated and supervised credit providers in Spain.
6. Spanish Mortgage Association (*Asociación Hipotecaria Española, AHE*): This association represents entities involved in mortgage

lending in Spain. It works to ensure best practices within the industry and compliance with regulatory standards, particularly those related to residential immovable property credit agreements.
7. Spanish Banking Association (*Asociación Española de Banca, AEB*): The AEB represents banks in Spain, providing a collective voice for its members in regulatory discussions and promoting best practices in banking, including the distribution of credit.

Open Access This chapter is licensed under the terms of the Creative Commons Attribution 4.0 International License (http://creativecommons.org/licenses/by/4.0/), which permits use, sharing, adaptation, distribution and reproduction in any medium or format, as long as you give appropriate credit to the original author(s) and the source, provide a link to the Creative Commons license and indicate if changes were made.

The images or other third party material in this chapter are included in the chapter's Creative Commons license, unless indicated otherwise in a credit line to the material. If material is not included in the chapter's Creative Commons license and your intended use is not permitted by statutory regulation or exceeds the permitted use, you will need to obtain permission directly from the copyright holder.

CHAPTER 8

United Kingdom

Abstract This chapter provides an overview of the UK credit intermediation framework, focusing on the Financial Conduct Authority (FCA) and the Prudential Regulation Authority (PRA). It discusses the licensing requirements, compliance obligations, and codes of conduct. The chapter highlights the UK's strong focus on consumer protection, transparency, and fair treatment, which set high professional standards for intermediaries.

Keywords United Kingdom • FCA • PRA • licensing • consumer credit • mortgage

The United Kingdom operates a complex system for governing credit intermediation with two distinct but not always separate regimes sitting side by side. Primary responsibility for regulating consumer credit intermediaries sits with the FCA, which sets out its requirements in the FCA Handbook, particularly the CONC (Consumer Credit Sourcebook) provisions. Similarly, mortgage intermediaries and lenders adhere to the FCA's MCOB (Mortgages and Home Finance: Conduct of Business) Handbook. The FCA derives its authority from the Financial Services and Markets Act (2000), FSMA, which also created the Financial Ombudsman

Service (FOS) to which consumers may refer complaints. Separately, the Consumer Credit Act 1974 also makes provisions governing consumer credit intermediaries and provides consumers with the right to seek redress through the courts. This chapter describes the regulatory architecture and the responsibilities of intermediaries in ensuring compliance, transparency and responsible lending.

Credit Intermediaries in the UK

In the United Kingdom, credit intermediaries are classified and regulated based on the specific type of credit product they handle.

Consumer credit intermediaries operate under the CONC[1], which governs activities such as personal loans and other short- to medium-term credit arrangements. Within this category, intermediaries are further divided into primary credit brokers (whose main business is credit broking) and secondary credit brokers (who engage in credit broking as an ancillary activity, such as car dealerships facilitating auto loans). Additionally, agents acting on behalf of firms engaged in credit-related activities are subject to specific FCA rules under CONC 2.5 (Conduct of Business: Credit Broking), CONC 4 (Pre-contractual requirements) and CONC 14 (Requirements in relation to agents), ensuring compliance with conduct and consumer protection regulations.

According to the Consumer Credit Act 1974, a credit intermediary is defined as a person or entity that, in the course of business and for financial compensation, engages in specific activities related to regulated consumer credit agreements, other than those secured on land. These activities include recommending or making available prospective credit agreements to individuals, assisting individuals with preparatory work for such agreements or entering into credit agreements on behalf of creditors. A credit intermediary does not act as a creditor but facilitates the process of obtaining credit for consumers.[2]

Below are outlined the different types of credit intermediaries regulated under the CONC and those governed by the MCD and MCOB.

---

[1] Since 2014
[2] Consumer Credit Act 1974, Part X, Section 160A

Definition of Credit Intermediaries – Consumer Credit Sourcebook (CONC): Credit Broker

According to CONC, a credit broker is a person who carries on an activity, by way of business, of the kind specified in Article 36A of the Regulated Activities Order.

The Financial Services and Markets Act 2000 (Regulated Activities) Order 2001[3], defines the following activities within credit broking:

1. *"effecting an introduction of an individual or relevant recipient of credit who wishes to enter into a credit agreement to a person ("P") with a view to P entering into by way of business as lender a regulated credit agreement (or an agreement which would be a regulated credit agreement but for any of the relevant provisions);*
2. *effecting an introduction of an individual or relevant recipient of credit who wishes to enter into a consumer hire agreement to a person ("P") with a view to P entering into by way of business as owner a regulated consumer hire agreement or an agreement which would be a regulated consumer hire agreement but for Article 60O (exempt agreements: exemptions relating to the nature of the agreement) or 60Q (exempt agreements: exemptions relating to the nature of the hirer);*
3. *effecting an introduction of an individual or relevant recipient of credit who wishes to enter into a credit agreement or consumer hire agreement (as the case may be) to a person who carries on an activity of the kind specified in sub-paragraph (a) or (b) by way of business;*
4. *presenting or offering an agreement which would (if entered into) be a regulated credit agreement (or an agreement which would be a regulated credit agreement but for any of the relevant provisions);*
5. *assisting an individual or relevant recipient of credit by undertaking preparatory work with a view to that person entering into a regulated credit agreement (or an agreement which would be a regulated credit agreement but for any of the relevant provisions);*
6. *entering into a regulated credit agreement (or an agreement which would be a regulated credit agreement but for any of the relevant provisions) on behalf of a lender."*

In the UK, there is a distinction between **Primary and Secondary Credit Brokers:**

---

[3] Art. 36A: https://www.legislation.gov.uk/uksi/2001/544/article/36A

- **Primary Credit Brokers** are financial intermediaries whose main business activity is helping customers identify and secure credit or hire agreements. Their role involves acting as a bridge between customers seeking financial products (such as loans, hire purchase agreements or consumer hire agreements) and the financial institutions or lenders providing them;
- **Secondary Credit Brokers** are entities or individuals for whom credit broking is not their primary business activity. Instead, they occasionally introduce customers to finance providers to facilitate transactions related to their main business. For example, a car dealership might introduce a customer to a lender to help finance the purchase of a car. This incidental involvement in credit broking is referred to as **secondary broking**.

Definition of Credit Intermediaries – Consumer Credit Sourcebook (CONC): Agents

Legislation in the UK related to agents mainly regulates the methods through which firms can appoint and supervise professionals who act as agents for credit-related activities. In this regard, the FCA regulates the appointment of agents for credit-related activities under CONC 14, with further detailed provisions in CONC 2.5 and CONC 4. These regimes establish detailed rules regarding the appointment, conduct and oversight of individuals acting as agents for credit-related activities, with firms held fully accountable for the conduct of their agents under provisions such as CONC 14.1.2R(5). Similarly, Section 56 of the Consumer Credit Act 1974 treats precontractual negotiations conducted by a credit broker with a potential client of the lender as though they were conducted by the lender itself, making them liable for any breaches of requirements by that broker.

A firm appointing an agent must ensure that the agent works exclusively for them and does not act on behalf of other principals. This exclusivity avoids potential conflicts of interest. This contract also requires the agent to inform customers that they are acting on behalf of the firm and to clearly disclose the firm's name.

The firm retains full responsibility for the actions of the agent when acting on its behalf. This includes treating any debt repayments collected by the agent as payments received directly by the firm. To ensure regulatory compliance, the firm must hold the necessary permissions for all activities the agent undertakes on its behalf[4].

---

[4] Part 4A of the Financial Services and Markets Act 2000 (Permission to carry on regulated activities).

Definition of Credit Intermediaries – *"Mortgages and Home Finance: Conduct of Business Sourcebook (MCOB)"*: *Mortgage Credit Intermediary*

Mortgage credit intermediaries in the UK are regulated under the FCA's MCOB rules. Although the UK has left the EU, key requirements from the MCD were retained post-Brexit and these were embedded into UK law via the European Union (Withdrawal) Act 2018 and subsequent statutory instruments. The FCA updated MCOB to reflect this shift by removing references to EU authorities but preserving the substantive obligations originally introduced by the MCD. These rules continue to govern both first and second charge regulated mortgage contracts, as well as consumer buy-to-let mortgages.

An MCD[5] mortgage credit intermediary refers to an entity involved in activities related to an MCD-regulated mortgage contract, as defined under the MCD. An **MCD mortgage credit intermediary** is an entity that operates under the full and unconditional responsibility of specific MCD mortgage lenders or groups. This intermediary may act on behalf of only one MCD mortgage lender, a single group, or a limited number of MCD mortgage lenders or groups, provided that this representation does not constitute the majority of the market.

This intermediary may act as either an MCD mortgage arranger, who facilitates the process of arranging mortgage contracts, or an MCD mortgage adviser, who provides personalised recommendations to consumers regarding such contracts. These roles are designed to ensure that intermediaries provide a clear and regulated service in assisting consumers with mortgage agreements, adhering to the standards outlined in Article 4(5) and (21) of the MCD.

An **MCD mortgage arranger** is a professional who, as part of their business and for financial remuneration (whether in monetary form or other agreed financial consideration), engages in activities specified in Article 25A(1)(a) or (2A)[6] of the Regulated Activities Order concerning MCD-regulated mortgage contracts. Their role involves more than simply introducing a consumer to an MCD firm; they actively participate in arranging the mortgage process.

---

[5] Mortgage Credit Directive

[6] 25A.- (1) Making arrangements – (a)for another person to enter into a regulated mortgage contract as borrower; (2A) making arrangements to enter into a regulated mortgage contract with a borrower on behalf of a lender is also a specified kind of activity.

An **MCD mortgage adviser**, on the other hand, provides personal recommendations to consumers regarding MCD-regulated mortgage contracts as part of their professional activities. Their role focuses on advising consumers based on their specific circumstances and needs, ensuring that recommendations are tailored and compliant with the provisions of Article 4(21) of the MCD.

In the UK, the MCOB rules apply to:

- **Regulated Mortgage Contracts**

    These are mortgages secured on a property in the UK where at least 40%[7] is used as the borrower's home. MCOB covers all stages of the process – disclosure, advice, affordability checks and post-sale conduct. Relevant sections include **MCOB 3, 4** and **11**.

- **Consumer Buy-to-Let Mortgages**

    These are buy-to-let loans where the borrower isn't acting mainly for business purposes, such as renting out a former home. They fall under regulation through the Mortgage Credit Directive Order 2015 and are treated like regulated mortgages under MCOB to ensure key consumer protections.

There are also a few retained requirements from the MCD that are embedded within the MCOB rules. These include:

- **Provision of the European Standardised Information Sheet (ESIS)**

    Required under **MCOB 5A.3**, the ESIS provides clear, comparable information on mortgage products, including interest rates, risks and total cost. It must be given early enough to enable informed decision-making.

- **Affordability and Creditworthiness Assessment**

    As per **MCOB 11.6.2R**, firms must carry out a thorough assessment of the consumer's ability to repay based on income, expenditure and other financial commitments. This includes verifying the information using reliable evidence. The assessment should not rely solely on property value increases.

- **Competency Requirements for Staff**

    Under **MCOB 2.8A**, firms must ensure that all relevant staff involved in mortgage activities have the appropriate knowledge and competence. This includes minimum qualifications (e.g. CeMAP or equivalent) and ongoing training.

---

[7] The Financial Services and Markets Act 2000, Art. 61(3).

- **Right of Reflection and Withdrawal**
  Consumers must be given a 7-day reflection period before accepting a binding offer (**MCOB 6A.3**), and a 14-day right to withdraw after conclusion, unless this right is lawfully waived in accordance with FCA rules.

These updates ensure that while the UK is no longer part of the EU, the principles and protections introduced by the MCD continue to form the foundation of UK mortgage regulation through a domestically governed framework.

Credit Intermediary and Licensing Requirements for Credit Intermediaries

The Threshold Conditions represent the minimum regulatory requirements that financial firms must satisfy to obtain and maintain authorisation under the Financial Services and Markets Act 2000 (FSMA) and are designed to ensure the stability, integrity, and effective supervision of financial institutions operating in the UK. Firms must demonstrate compliance with these conditions at all times, ensuring that they remain financially sound, well-governed, and capable of operating within the expectations of the regulatory environment.

The detailed application of Threshold Conditions varies depending on whether the firm is regulated by the FCA, the Prudential Regulation Authority (PRA) or by both regulators under a system known in the UK as dual regulation[8].

Each condition addresses a key aspect of financial regulation, including:

1. location of Offices – Ensuring that firms have a registered office and head office within the UK to allow for effective regulatory oversight: The Location of Offices threshold condition, as set out in

---

[8] For further information:

1. Bank of England note on PRA and FCA threshold Conditions – https://www.bankofengland.co.uk/-/media/boe/files/prudential-regulation/new-bank/thresholdconditionsfactsheet#:~:text=There%20are%20a%20number%20of,in%20the%20interests%20of%20consumers;
2. FCA threshold conditions in COND - https://www.handbook.fca.org.uk/handbook/COND/1/?view=chapter
3. To read COND as a whole document click here: https://www.handbook.fca.org.uk/handbook/COND.pdf

Paragraph 2B of Schedule 6 to the Financial Services and Markets Act 2000 (FSMA), requires that financial firms carrying out regulated activities in the United Kingdom have their head office and, where applicable, their registered office within the UK. The requirement applies to all firms seeking permission to carry out regulated activities, and it ensures they maintain a physical and operational presence within the UK financial system.

2. Effective Supervision – Requiring firms to be structured in a way that enables clear regulatory monitoring, particularly in cases involving complex group structures or cross-border operations: The Effective Supervision condition requires that firms be structured in a way that allows for clear and continuous regulatory oversight by the FCA. The complexity of a firm's business operations, financial products, and corporate structure is assessed to determine whether the FCA can effectively monitor its activities.

3. Appropriate Resources – Mandating that firms possess adequate financial and non-financial resources, including capital reserves, liquidity, and risk management capabilities: the Appropriate Resources condition ensures that firms possess sufficient financial and non-financial resources to sustain their operations and meet regulatory requirements. The FCA evaluates a firm's capital adequacy, liquidity provisions, and ability to manage financial risks, ensuring that it can meet debt obligations and regulatory capital requirements[9]. Non-financial resources include risk management systems, governance frameworks and human resources capable of ensuring compliance with regulatory and prudential standards. The FCA also considers the firm's ability to withstand economic shocks, maintain continuity in service delivery and address potential risks associated with its business activities. If a firm is part of a financial group, the FCA may assess the financial strength of the group to determine whether its resources are sufficient to support the firm's obligations.

4. Suitability – Establishing that firms and their management teams are fit and proper, with the necessary expertise, integrity and governance structures to operate responsibly: the Suitability condition requires that firms and their senior management teams demonstrate the

---

[9] Although the FCA does consider the appropriate resources, checks on capital adequacy and liquidity are more commonly associated with the PRA. COND 2.4.2G(2) suggests that FCA will only check for these things if the firm is not also regulated by the PRA.

necessary integrity, competence and governance structures to operate in a regulated environment. Firms must conduct their business in a manner that aligns with consumer protection principles, market transparency and financial crime prevention regulations. The FCA evaluates whether key individuals within the firm have the experience and qualifications necessary to manage regulated activities, as well as whether the firm has a history of compliance with financial regulations. If a firm or its senior executives have previously been subject to regulatory sanctions, criminal proceedings or enforcement actions, these factors will influence the FCA's assessment of suitability. The FCA also considers whether the firm has robust internal controls, risk management procedures and ethical business practices to ensure ongoing compliance with regulatory standards.
5. Business Model – Ensuring that a firm's business model is viable, sustainable and aligned with the interests of financial stability and consumer protection: the Business Model condition assesses whether a firm's strategic approach and operational framework are viable, sustainable and aligned with financial stability objectives. The FCA evaluates whether a firm's business strategy is consistent with prudent risk management and consumer protection principles. A firm's profitability, financial resilience and adaptability to market changes are critical considerations in assessing whether its business model is sustainable. Additionally, the FCA examines external factors such as macroeconomic conditions, regulatory changes and industry developments that may impact the firm's long-term viability. Firms must also demonstrate that they have contingency plans in place to address potential risks, including financial crises, operational disruptions and regulatory changes.

Laws and Relevant Authorities in the UK

In the UK, firms providing financial services must be authorised by the FCA or registered with it. The FCA is the independent regulatory body responsible for overseeing the conduct of approximately 42,000 financial services firms and markets in the United Kingdom. Its operational objectives are protecting consumers by safeguarding them from harm caused by poor practices within the financial services sector, enhancing market integrity to promote a healthy, stable, and successful financial system, promoting effective competition in the interests of consumers and addressing anti-competitive practices.

The regime for regulating professional conduct standards for financial agents and credit brokers in the UK is complex and fragmented. There are four main legal sources in the UK:

1. **Direct Regulation by the FCA**

The FCA enforces at least three overlapping regulatory frameworks for lenders and intermediaries:
- Behaviour- or conduct-based regulation (e.g., CONC, MCOBS),
- Outcomes-based regulation (e.g., Consumer Duty), and
- Principles-based regulation (e.g., PRIN 6).
- Specific provisions apply to the appointment of agents for credit-related regulated activities, as outlined in CONC 14, which requires firms to:
  - take full responsibility for the conduct of their agents (CONC 14.1.2 R(5));
  - implement measures to ensure compliance by agents (CONC 14.1.4R).
- There are also other detailed requirements, such as CONC 2.5, which sets out specific conduct of business requirements related to credit broking, and CONC 4 covering pre-contractual requirements, which also have extensive rules to which credit brokers must adhere.

2. **The Consumer Credit Act 1974 (CCA)**

Before the establishment of the FCA in 2014, consumer protection in credit markets was primarily governed by the Consumer Credit Act 1974 (CCA). The Financial Services Act 2012, which amended the Financial Services and Markets Act 2000 (FSMA), transferred some – but not all – consumer protection provisions from the CCA to the FCA Handbook. This shift aimed to enable quicker updates to consumer protections by empowering the FCA to make rules rather than relying on parliamentary amendments. One of the most important provisions remaining in the CCA is Section 56, which covers Antecedent negotiations. The practical effect of this section is to make the credit broker a deemed agent of the lender in relation to such negotiations, making lenders responsible for any breaches by them.

3. **Voluntary Standards**

Voluntary standards provide an additional level of governance, promoting adherence to best practices that exceed minimum legal and regulatory requirements.

4. The Competition Act 1998

The Competition Act 1998, alongside Articles 81 and 82 of the EC Treaty, prohibits anti-competitive agreements and abuse of market dominance. Financial services firms are particularly vigilant regarding compliance with competition rules, as intermediaries face severe penalties for anti-competitive behaviour.

For the purposes of the present work, mainly the FCA Handbook will be considered as the primary source of regulatory standards and guidance.

The FCA Handbook encompasses a wide range of provisions that regulate the activities of financial agents and credit brokers, including, but not limited to, behavioural, outcomes-based and principles-based regulations. Main sections of the Handbook, such as the Consumer Credit Sourcebook (CONC), the Mortgages and Home Finance: Conduct of Business Sourcebook (MCOBS), and the Principles for Businesses (PRIN), offer detailed requirements and expectations that firms must adhere to in their professional conduct.

Regulation by the FCA. Behaviour- or Conduct-Based Regulation: The Consumer Credit Sourcebook (CONC)

The Consumer Credit sourcebook (CONC) serves as the specialist sourcebook for consumer credit-related regulated activities. Its application is as described in this section, unless otherwise specified in the individual sections or rules within CONC.

The purpose of CONC is to outline the detailed obligations specific to consumer credit-related regulated activities and associated activities carried out by firms. These obligations build upon and expand the high-level requirements set out in other parts of the FCA Handbook, such as the Principles for Businesses (PRIN), the General Provisions (GEN) and the Senior Management Arrangements, Systems and Controls (SYSC), as well as those stipulated under the Consumer Credit Act (CCA)[10].

CONC does not apply to credit agreements secured on land, with some limited exceptions.

---

[10] For more information on the Senior Managers and Certification Regime (SMCR), see: Financial Conduct Authority, *Senior Managers and Certification Regime (SM&CR)*, available at https://www.fca.org.uk/firms/senior-managers-certification-regime (accessed 13 June 2025).

Regulation by the FCA. Behaviour- or Conduct-Based Regulation: The Mortgages and Home Finance: Conduct of Business Sourcebook (MCOB)

The Mortgages and Home Finance: Conduct of Business Sourcebook (MCOB) establishes a conduct-based framework for firms engaged in home finance activities. The purpose of MCOB is to define to whom and for what activities its rules apply, as well as the territorial limits of these regulations.MCOB applies to all firms conducting home finance activities, including regulated mortgage contracts, equity release transactions, home purchase plans and regulated sale and rent back agreements. It also extends to firms that communicate or approve financial promotions for these products. Firms outsourcing regulated activities to third-party processors remain fully responsible for compliance with MCOB, ensuring that consumers are always aware of the firm's identity as the responsible entity. The sourcebook categorises firms into lenders/providers, administrators, arrangers and advisers, with arrangers and advisers collectively referred to as intermediaries. Activities are broadly classified as home finance transactions, including lifetime mortgages, home reversion plans, equity release transactions and sale and rent back agreements. Detailed guidance on these classifications and their applications is provided in the FCA's Perimeter Guidance Manual (PERG). For business loans and loans to high-net-worth mortgage customers, MCOB provides tailored provisions. Firms must either comply fully with MCOB or adhere to MCOB with tailored adjustments specific to these categories. High-net-worth mortgage customers include individuals meeting specific financial criteria, and the tailored provisions apply even in joint borrower situations if one borrower qualifies as high net worth. Certain provisions of MCOB apply specifically to high-net-worth mortgage customers and business-purpose transactions. These tailored and universal provisions aim to accommodate specific customer needs while ensuring robust consumer protection. The overarching goal of MCOB is to promote ethical conduct, ensure consumer confidence and maintain market integrity in home finance activities.

Regulation by the FCA Outcomes-Based Regulation: The Consumer Duty

The Consumer Duty – which came into force for open products and services on 31 July 2023 – introduced an outcomes-based regulatory framework aimed at elevating the standards of care and protection provided to retail consumers in financial markets. This approach emphasises the results that firms achieve for their customers rather than solely focusing on adherence to prescriptive rules. The Duty requires firms to prioritise delivering good outcomes across all stages of the consumer relationship, involving product design, pricing, communications and support services. Under this framework, firms are expected to integrate the Duty's principles into their operations dynamically, responding effectively to evolving market conditions, technological innovations and consumer behaviours. Outcomes-based regulation requires firms to adapt their practices to meet the needs of their customers.

The Duty comprises a Consumer Principle, cross-cutting rules and four specific outcomes, which collectively define the FCA's expectations. These outcomes address the governance of products and services, the fair value of offerings, consumer understanding and the quality of support provided to customers. Firms are required to adopt a proactive stance, continuously evaluating whether their activities result in positive customer experiences and adjusting practices where deficiencies are identified. This approach attempts to balance innovation, enabling firms to develop new products and services while ensuring robust consumer protection. It also seeks to enable the FCA to monitor and intervene promptly, identifying and mitigating potential harms before they escalate. The Duty aligns regulatory objectives with the broader goal of promoting trust and confidence in financial markets, focusing on tangible consumer outcomes.

Regulation by the FCA. Principles-Based Regulation: The Principles

The Principles represent a general statement of the core obligations of firms and other applicable entities under the regulatory system. Their authority stems from the FCA's rule-making powers as set out in the Financial Services and Markets Act (FSMA), the Payment Services Regulations and the Electronic Money Regulations. The Principles align with the FCA's statutory objectives and provide a high-level framework for expected behaviours and standards.

The Principles for Businesses (PRIN) outlined by the FCA set the foundation for the conduct and responsibilities of regulated firms. These principles establish high-level standards that firms must adhere to in their operations, ensuring integrity, fairness and accountability in the financial services industry. There are 12 Principles, as follows:

1. Integrity: Firms must conduct their business with honesty and integrity, ensuring trustworthiness in their dealings.
2. Skill, Care and Diligence: Firms are required to operate with due skill, care, and diligence, reflecting professionalism in all activities.
3. Management and Control: Firms must take reasonable care to organise and control their affairs responsibly and implement effective risk management systems.
4. Financial Prudence: Adequate financial resources must be maintained to ensure stability and compliance with obligations.
5. Market Conduct: Proper standards of market conduct must be observed to uphold fair and efficient financial markets.
6. Customers' Interests: Firms must prioritise the interests of their customers, ensuring fair treatment across all interactions and services.
7. Communications with Clients: Information provided to clients must be clear, fair and not misleading, addressing their needs effectively.
8. Conflicts of Interest: Firms must manage conflicts of interest fairly, both between themselves and their customers, and between customers and other clients.
9. Customers – Relationships of Trust: Firms must ensure the suitability of their advice and discretionary decisions for customers who rely on their judgement.
10. Clients' Assets: Adequate protection must be arranged for clients' assets when the firm is responsible for them.
11. Relations with Regulators: Firms must engage with regulators in an open and cooperative manner, disclosing relevant information that the regulator would reasonably expect to be notified of.
12. Consumer Duty: Firms must act to deliver good outcomes for retail customers, reflecting a heightened focus on consumer protection and satisfaction.

These Principles, within the FCA's regulatory framework, guide firms in their conduct and interactions with customers, the market, and regulators.

The Consumer Credit Act 1974

The Consumer Credit Act of 1974 (CCA) was the primary piece of legislation protecting consumers in credit transactions before the FCA was established in 2014. While some of its provisions were transferred to the FCA's rulebook, others remained within the CCA, such as Sections 56 and 140A. Section 56 holds lenders accountable for the actions of brokers and agents during pre-contract negotiations. It effectively treats these intermediaries as agents of the lender, even if they are not formally employed by them. This means that lenders can be held liable for any misrepresentations or unfair practices committed by these intermediaries. Section 140A addresses unfair relationships between creditors and debtors. It allows courts to intervene if they find that a creditor has acted unfairly, even if the specific behaviour isn't explicitly prohibited by law. This broad power gives courts significant discretion to protect consumers from harmful practices. The CCA empowers lenders to exert control over their intermediaries to mitigate the risk of liability. This indirect regulatory influence supplements the direct oversight provided by the FCA. By carefully selecting and monitoring their intermediaries, lenders attempt to minimise the chances of legal issues arising from unfair practices or misrepresentations.

Voluntary Standards

Voluntary standards offer an additional layer of quality control beyond legal and regulatory requirements. These standards often represent industry best practices. For instance, the FLA Lending Code outlines commitments that all FLA members must adhere to. This includes guidelines for intermediaries, which lenders can enforce by refusing to work with those that do not comply. In the UK motor finance sector, almost all lenders are FLA members and require their distributors to be "SAF Approved" or hold a similar qualification. The Specialist Automotive Finance (SAF) scheme, established by the FLA in 2007, is an annual learning programme and assessment of competence in motor finance for customer-facing staff in the industry.. This certification is necessary for dealers, lenders, and brokers alike. While ethical and business reasons drive the demand for SAF accreditation, it is also important for regulatory compliance. Lenders can rely on SAF to ensure that their products are distributed responsibly by intermediaries. SAF recognises other accreditations that meet its standards.

The Competition Act 1998

In the UK, anti-competitive behaviour is strictly prohibited under both domestic and European Union law. The Competition Act 1998 and

Articles 81 and 82 of the EC Treaty prohibit anti-competitive agreements between businesses and the abuse of a dominant market position. Financial services firms in the UK are acutely aware of these regulations and take significant steps to ensure compliance. Intermediaries, in particular, must carefully avoid any practices that could be deemed anti-competitive, as such actions can lead to severe penalties.

Open Access This chapter is licensed under the terms of the Creative Commons Attribution 4.0 International License (http://creativecommons.org/licenses/by/4.0/), which permits use, sharing, adaptation, distribution and reproduction in any medium or format, as long as you give appropriate credit to the original author(s) and the source, provide a link to the Creative Commons license and indicate if changes were made.

The images or other third party material in this chapter are included in the chapter's Creative Commons license, unless indicated otherwise in a credit line to the material. If material is not included in the chapter's Creative Commons license and your intended use is not permitted by statutory regulation or exceeds the permitted use, you will need to obtain permission directly from the copyright holder.

CHAPTER 9

Comparative Analysis

Abstract This chapter synthesizes findings from the national chapters and offers a comparative analysis of the regulatory frameworks governing credit intermediation in Europe. It identifies key similarities and major differences among factors such as licensing requirements, professional standards, and transparency obligations, as well as supervisory structures. The chapter discusses challenges common across jurisdictions, including regulatory fragmentation, compliance costs, and the need to adapt to digital innovation. It also highlights best practices and potential pathways toward greater harmonization within the EU framework.

Keywords comparative analysis • credit intermediation • EU regulation • licensing • supervision • harmonization • best practices

The regulation of credit intermediaries across Europe reflects a converging framework but is still far from total harmonisation, formed by different national laws, diverse supervisory authorities and distinct market structures. This comparative analysis explores the regulatory frameworks of European countries (Italy, France, Germany, Spain, Belgium, Portugal) and the United Kingdom, focusing on the main characteristics of credit intermediation, licensing requirements, and relevant legal and institutional authorities. Different regulatory principles and national specificities influence the operation and supervision of credit intermediaries.

Italy represents a structured and formalised system of credit intermediation, supervised by the OAM and governed by Legislative Decree 141/2010. The distinction between agents and brokers is fundamental in the Italian system, with both roles subject to mandatory registration, professional training, and continuous professional development. Italy's approach is notably influenced by a strong emphasis on consumer protection and the prevention of conflicts of interest, especially in the mortgage and consumer lending segments. The OAM serves not only as a registration authority but also as a supervisory body, thereby consolidating oversight and reinforcing compliance among intermediaries.

France adopts a similarly formal framework through the registration of credit intermediaries with ORIAS, under the regulatory guidance of the ACPR[1]. The French regime incorporates four categories of credit intermediaries under the IOBSP (*Intermédiaires en Opérations de Banque et en Services de Paiement*) classification. The distinction is made between brokers, who are under the direct control of the ACPR (the supervisory authority). They must belong to an approved professional association, which guarantees their compliance with the rules, and agents, considered as essential outsourced service providers, who are under the control of their principals, credit institutions or financing companies (internal control). This stratified structure reflects the complexity of the financial intermediation ecosystem in France, where entities range from insurance brokers to specialised lending intermediaries. The requirement for professional indemnity insurance and demonstrable financial capability underscores a risk-based approach to regulation. France's Monetary and Financial Code, complemented by sector-specific rules, ensures that intermediary activity aligns with national financial stability and consumer protection objectives.

In Germany, credit intermediaries do not conduct lending business within the meaning of the German Banking Act (Kreditwesengesetz, KWG). They do not grant credits themselves, but support entering into credit contracts on behalf of borrowers (individual or firm) or credit providers. Credit intermediation does not constitute banking or financial services business according to the Banking Act. The German Banking Supervisory

---

[1] Autorité de contrôle prudentiel et de résolution

Authority (BaFin) is not the supervisory authority for credit intermediaries. The Trade Supervisory Authorities of the federal states (*Bundesländer*) are responsible for supervising credit intermediaries (financial agents and credit brokers). This also applies to online loan comparison platforms or loan brokerage platforms that arrange bank loans (intermediary websites). Credit intermediaries in Germany must meet fit and proper standards and operate within a legal environment that prioritises transparency and systemic risk mitigation. The result is a system in which intermediaries are often viewed as an extension of the regulated financial sector.

In Spain, consumer credit distribution and brokerage between entities and consumers, as well as the granting of credit, are not reserved activities for supervised institutions. Therefore, these activities can be carried out by natural or legal persons, different from financial institutions, that usually combine these activities with other activities such as advisory or agency. So, consumer credit intermediaries, different from residential immovable property credit intermediaries, are not required to register, nor are they supervised by the Bank of Spain.

Within the real estate area, intermediaries are supervised. The Spanish model mandates training and certification for intermediaries, and this approach reflects a competence-based regulatory philosophy. The emphasis on professional qualifications is intended to enhance the quality of intermediation services and safeguard consumers from mis-selling and credit-related abuses. Spain's framework also requires civil liability insurance, aligning with the broader European framework and reinforcing financial responsibility. The role of the Bank of Spain encompasses licensing, oversight and enforcement functions, which contribute to the regulatory environment. Regarding consumer protection, the Spanish law assigned the management of the State Registry to the General Subdirectorate of Consumer Quality of the National Consumer Institute. Currently, these responsibilities are exercised by the governing bodies within the Ministry of Consumption.

Belgium, under the authority of the FSMA, employs a regulatory model that requires registration procedures to obtain accreditation. The Belgian CEL and Royal decree of 29 October 2015 provide a comprehensive legal foundation for the supervision of credit intermediaries. The FSMA's focus extends beyond compliance monitoring to include educational initiatives aimed at enhancing intermediary competence and ethical standards. Belgium's integration of anti-money laundering (AML) and counter-terrorist financing (CFT) obligations into the credit intermediation framework illustrates a holistic approach to regulatory policy. This integration ensures that credit intermediaries contribute to the integrity of the financial system while fulfilling their commercial functions.

Portugal's regime is governed by Decree-Law No. 81-C/2017 and supervised by the Bank of Portugal. The Portuguese model mandates professional training and adherence to fit and proper requirements for all credit intermediaries. The regulatory emphasis on professionalisation and ethical behaviour aligns with European supervisory trends. Bank of Portugal performs both a licensing and monitoring role, ensuring that intermediaries operate within a well-defined legal framework.

The United Kingdom, while no longer an EU member state, remains an important comparative case study due to its economic relevance and proximity, and for its regulatory model under the FCA. Firms providing financial services in the UK need to be authorised by the FCA. The UK's framework places considerable weight on consumer outcomes, fair treatment and clear communication. The FCA's rules mandate strict conduct requirements, including affordability assessments, product suitability and transparency in fees and commissions.

Across these jurisdictions, common principles emerge. First, all countries provide a legal framework often involving fit and proper assessments, professional training and financial responsibility, even if not all of them require stringent registration or licensing of credit intermediaries. Second, there is a strong emphasis on consumer protection, especially through rules on transparency, conflict of interest management and product suitability. These shared principles reflect the influence of EU directives, like the MCD, which has harmonised certain aspects of credit intermediation across the market.

However, national differences persist and are influenced by the historical evolution of financial systems and domestic regulatory philosophies. The regulatory supervision bodies are different: in certain cases, the supervision is made by the national central bank, in other cases, countries have a specific authority specialised in the field.

These variations can have significant implications for cross-border credit intermediation, especially in the context of the EU single market. Divergences in training requirements, licensing procedures and supervision intensity may create barriers to entry and complicate passporting arrangements.

A potential area for further harmonisation lies in the creation of interoperable and centralised databases of authorised intermediaries in the EU.

The regulation of credit intermediaries in Europe is marked by a still significant difference between harmonisation and national discretion. While EU-level directives provide a common foundation, the implementation of these rules varies significantly across member states and the UK. This comparative analysis reveals that some countries adopt specific and specialised supervisory bodies and ask for specific licensing requirements, while others are still consolidating their frameworks. The convergence toward best practices in licensing, training and consumer protection is evident, yet the diversity in institutional arrangements suggests that a one-size-fits-all model remains elusive. Ongoing dialogue among regulators, hopefully supported by research such as the OAM's European Study on Credit Distribution, is essential to contribute to a balanced and effective regulatory ecosystem that protects consumers while promoting innovation and financial inclusion, as well as fair and equal treatment across Europe for professional figures like agents and brokers.

These findings are synthesized in Table 1, which summarizes for each country the main categories of credit intermediaries, licensing requirements, and applicable laws and supervisory authorities, providing a reference to the comparative analysis presented above.

Table 1 Summary of the Comparative Analysis

Country	Credit Intermediaries – Key Points	Main Licensing Requirements	Main Laws and Relevant Authorities
Italy	Credit intermediaries must be registered with and supervised by OAM, and categorised as agents or brokers. **Categories**: Agents (on behalf of financial institutions); Brokers (independent)	Mandatory registration with OAM; different requirements for agents and brokers, including fit and proper tests. **Licensing requirements for agents (natural persons)**: high school diploma, domicile in Italy, good reputation, professional exam **Licensing requirements for agents (legal entity)**: registered and administrative headquarters or, for EU entities, permanent establishment in the territory of the Republic, requirements of good repute and professionalism and civil liability insurance policy **Licensing requirements for brokers**: Professionalism; honourability; capital requirement; technical-IT	**Law**: Legislative Decree 141/2010; **Authority**: OAM (Organismo Agenti e Mediatori).
France	Credit intermediaries operate under the supervision of ORIAS. **Categories**: Broker, Exclusive Agent, Non-Exclusive Agent, Agent of an Intermediary	ORIAS registration, proof of good repute, professionalism and financial capacity; applies to IOBSPs (*intermédiaires*). Need professional indemnity insurance in certain cases.	**Law**: Monetary and Financial Code and Consumer Credit Rules; **Authority**: ORIAS and ACPR.

Germany	Intermediaries do not require registration with BaFin; the Trade Supervisory Authorities of the federal states (Bundesländer) are responsible for supervising credit intermediaries (financial agents and credit brokers) **Categories**: Financial agents, Credit brokers, Retailers at point-of-sale	Licensing requirement under Section 34c of the Trade, Commerce and Industry Regulation Act (Gewerbeordnung, GewO). Credit intermediaries operating in the mortgage credit market need a special license under Section 34i GewO in conjunction with the German Mortgage Credit Mediation Ordinance (Verordnung über Immobiliardarlehensvermittlung). **Licensing requirements**: evidence of the trustworthiness and of the good repute, adequate financial resources, evidence of appropriate knowledge and competence with regard to credit products and services (this means minimum standards/qualifications needed to begin acting as an intermediary); credit intermediaries operating in the mortgage credit market have to provide a certificate of competence, in order to obtain the administrative license for their services. Credit intermediaries operating in the mortgage credit market have to register in the brokerage register before starting business.	**Law**: Trade, Commerce and Industry Regulation Act (Gewerbeordnung, GewO); **Authority**: Trade Supervisory Authorities of the federal states (Bundesländer)
Spain	Consumer credit intermediaries, different from residential immovable property credit intermediaries, are not required to register, nor are they supervised by the Bank of Spain. **Categories**: Tied Intermediary, Appointed Representative	Bank of Spain supervises intermediaries active in the real estate sector; registration in the appropriate registry requires prior verification by the competent authority to ensure compliance with legal and regulatory requirements. Licensing requirements (Only for Real Estate): Technical capacity, financial guarantees, anti-money laundering compliance, training plan	**Law**: Law 5/2019, Royal Decree 106/2011, Law 16/2011; **Authority**: Bank of Spain.

(continued)

Table 1 (continued)

Belgium	FSMA registers intermediaries. **Categories**: *Mortgage*: Credit broker, Tied agent, Subagent; *Consumer*: Credit broker, Tied agent, Ancillary agent	Must register with FSMA and complete training. **Licensing requirements**: Professional knowledge, expertise, integrity, liability insurance, declaration of independence from exclusive agreements	**Law**: Book VII of the Code of Economic Law (CEL), Royal decree of 29 October 2015, Royal decree regulating the spread of the commission for mediation on credit agreements; **Authority**: Financial Services and Markets Authority (FSMA) and the Federal Public Service Finances (FPS – Service public fédéral Finances)
Portugal	Bank of Portugal oversees intermediaries; registration and training are required. **Categories**: Ancillary Intermediary, Tied Intermediary, Untied Intermediary	Registration with the Bank of Portugal; fit and proper requirements and professional training are mandatory. **Licensing requirements** (for natural person): Nationality, legal capacity, suitability, knowledge of credit law, proper organisation, liability insurance **Licensing requirements** (for legal entity): Shareholding Requirements, Employee Knowledge Requirements and Technical Manager Requirements. Additionally, intermediaries are required to have professional liability insurance to cover potential civil liabilities arising from professional negligence. For untied intermediaries: sole corporate purpose must be the activity of credit intermediation, capital may not include participation from credit institutions, financial companies, payment institutions, electronic money institutions, tied credit intermediaries or ancillary credit intermediaries.	**Law**: Decree-Law No. 81-C/2017; Decree-Law 133/2009; Notice of Bank of Portugal 6/2017 **Authority**: Bank of Portugal.

United Kingdom	Credit intermediaries operate under the Financial Conduct Authority (FCA). **Categories**: Primary and Secondary Credit Brokers (CONC); Agents (CONC); Arranger, Adviser (MCOB)	Must be authorised by the FCA; requires adherence to conduct rules, disclosure and fair treatment of customers. The Threshold Conditions represent the minimum regulatory requirements that financial firms must satisfy to obtain and maintain authorisation under the Financial Conduct Authority (FCA) and the Prudential Regulation Authority (PRA). **Licensing requirements**: location of offices, effective supervision, appropriate resources, suitability, business model	**Law**: *Direct regulation by the FCA* [behaviour or conduct-based regulation (e.g. CONC, MCOBS), outcomes-based regulation (e.g. Consumer Duty) and principles-based (e.g. PRIN 6)], *Consumer Credit Act 1974, Voluntary standards, Competition Act 1998* **Authority**: Financial Conduct Authority (FCA) and Prudential Regulation Authority (PRA).

Open Access This chapter is licensed under the terms of the Creative Commons Attribution 4.0 International License (http://creativecommons.org/licenses/by/4.0/), which permits use, sharing, adaptation, distribution and reproduction in any medium or format, as long as you give appropriate credit to the original author(s) and the source, provide a link to the Creative Commons license and indicate if changes were made.

The images or other third party material in this chapter are included in the chapter's Creative Commons license, unless indicated otherwise in a credit line to the material. If material is not included in the chapter's Creative Commons license and your intended use is not permitted by statutory regulation or exceeds the permitted use, you will need to obtain permission directly from the copyright holder.

CHAPTER 10

Conclusions

Abstract The concluding chapter reflects on the study's findings, emphasizing the importance of credit intermediaries in facilitating access to credit and supporting market efficiency. It highlights the need for balanced regulatory frameworks that protect consumers while ensuring competitive and innovative market practices. The chapter discusses the implications of regulatory diversity for cross- border operations, the potential benefits of harmonization, and the continuing evolution of European and UK frameworks. Finally, it suggests areas for future research, including the impact of fintech considerations on credit distribution.

Keywords conclusions • credit intermediation • consumer protection • regulation • harmonization • fintech • innovation

Loan distribution in Europe has a crucial role in defining the region's financial ecosystem, serving as the mechanism through which banks, non-bank institutions and intermediaries channel funds to businesses and consumers. Traditionally, European banks have played a dominant role in lending, relying on established relationships and local market knowledge. However, the landscape has evolved significantly due to international competition, the rise of non-traditional players, such as fintech companies and the developments of e-commerce.

This evolution has been driven by both technological advancements and regulatory reforms. Digital interfaces have enabled quicker loan processing and decision-making, often by using data analytics and artificial intelligence to assess borrower creditworthiness. Concurrently, regulatory efforts aimed at harmonising standards – although varied across member states – have improved transparency and consumer protection. These measures ensure that loan distribution not only supports economic growth but also maintains financial stability and safeguards against excessive risk-taking, and at the same time guarantees consumer protection.

In this evolving scenario, the loan distribution sector in Europe faces several challenges. The regulatory framework, despite the European Union initiatives, remains somewhat fragmented across different jurisdictions, making cross-border operations complex. Additionally, the rapid pace of technological change requires continuous adaptation by financial institutions to remain competitive and compliant. Balancing innovation with the need for robust consumer protection remains an ongoing concern for policymakers and industry stakeholders alike.

It is therefore evident that loan distribution in Europe is undergoing transformative change: the integration of digital solutions and new market entrants is reshaping the way loans are distributed. This dynamic environment, supported by evolving regulatory frameworks, holds the promise of enhanced efficiency and broader financial inclusion, provided that the challenges of regulatory diversity and technological disruption are effectively managed.

In this scenario, the role of more traditional credit intermediaries, such as agents and credit brokers, has to be investigated to understand their role and positioning in an increasingly competitive and integrated market.

This study provides an extensive analysis of the credit distribution by agents and brokers in Europe, examining the regulatory frameworks, operational structures, and market dynamics across key jurisdictions, including Belgium, France, Germany, Italy, Portugal, Spain and the United Kingdom.

The main finding of the study is that, particularly in this domain, the diversity and fragmentation of regulatory frameworks governing credit intermediation persists. The MCD and the CCD have greatly contributed to the creation of a Single Market in retail lending; however, when it comes to credit distribution, national differences remain. Each country has developed its own licensing regimes, professional standards and supervisory mechanisms aimed at ensuring transparency, consumer protection and market integrity.

Key challenges identified include not only the persistent fragmentation of regulatory environments, but also the need for continuous professional updating in the face of rapid technological advancements and regulatory change; finding the right balance point between innovation and stringent consumer protection is also a demanding but necessary task. Despite these challenges, the study highlights significant opportunities for credit intermediaries provided they preserve and enhance their role as suppliers of customised and value-added services to borrowers and lenders.

Some threats, however, must be considered, the main one being the impact in terms of efficiency, cost and immediateness of online solutions. Comparing the two models can help us identify the advantages and disadvantages of the two alternatives.

Online credit channels leverage technology to streamline the loan application process. These platforms use digital algorithms, data analytics and sometimes artificial intelligence to quickly assess creditworthiness and match borrowers with appropriate lenders. The process is generally fast, transparent, and accessible from anywhere with an internet connection. This efficiency often translates into competitive pricing compared to traditional methods. However, while online channels offer convenience and speed, they may lack the personalised guidance of a human advisor, and the digital interface might not fully address the unique needs of every borrower, particularly those with complex financial situations.

On the other side, credit intermediaries such as agents and brokers provide personalised advice and help borrowers navigate complex loan products. Their deep industry knowledge and established relationships can be especially valuable for those with unique financial situations or credit histories. However, the interaction might involve more in-person consultations and paperwork, and services usually come with fees or commissions that can affect the overall cost of borrowing.

In a nutshell:

- **Personalisation vs. Efficiency:** Credit intermediaries offer personalised service and tailored advice, which can be beneficial for borrowers with complex financial profiles. In contrast, online channels emphasise efficiency and speed, ideal for borrowers seeking quick approvals.

- **Cost:** The fee structures differ; credit intermediaries may charge commissions that increase overall borrowing costs, whereas online channels often boast lower fees due to automation.
- **Accessibility:** Online channels provide round-the-clock access and a user-friendly interface, making them accessible to a broader audience. Agents and brokers, though sometimes more limited in availability, can offer a human touch that reassures and educates borrowers.

The choice between using a loan broker or an online interface largely depends on the borrower's individual needs. Borrowers who value personalised advice and have complex financial profiles may benefit from engaging a loan broker, while those seeking a quick, streamlined process with competitive rates might prefer the convenience of an online interface. This is the everlasting tug of war between what is generally labelled as *high touch* compared with *high tech* distribution, with the latter increasingly challenging the former.

This evolution in distribution models reflects broader trends in consumer behaviour, technological advancement and regulatory change. Balancing these two approaches is critical as financial institutions strive to deliver value, enhance customer experience and maintain operational efficiency.

Historically, financial services distribution relied heavily on personal interactions. Advisors, relationship managers, branch staff and also agents and brokers played a crucial role in building trust and understanding clients' unique financial needs.

This "high touch" model, which characterises credit intermediaries, has several advantages; by acting as intermediaries between borrowers and lenders, agents and credit brokers play a pivotal role in ensuring that consumers have access to the most suitable credit products available. Their strong points are multifaceted, spanning from personalised service and industry expertise to market flexibility and enhanced transparency.

One of the key strengths is the ability to offer personalised guidance. Unlike standardised online channels, credit intermediaries take the time to understand the unique financial situations, credit histories, and specific needs of each client. This tailored approach enables them to match borrowers with credit products that best suit their circumstances, whether that involves finding a competitive interest rate or selecting a loan with flexible repayment options. The human touch inherent in this process fosters trust and builds long-term relationships with clients, enhancing customer satisfaction and loyalty.

Agent and credit brokers possess deep industry knowledge, honed through years of experience and continuous learning. Their expertise allows them to navigate the complexities of the credit market, which includes a wide range of loan products, lending criteria and regulatory requirements. This extensive market knowledge not only enables them to identify the best lending options but also to negotiate favourable terms on behalf of their clients. Furthermore, agents and brokers typically maintain robust relationships with a variety of financial institutions, ensuring that they can offer borrowers access to multiple lenders and a broader spectrum of credit solutions.

Another strong point of credit intermediaries is the efficiency they bring to the credit acquisition process. For many borrowers, particularly those with complex financial profiles, the task of researching and comparing various loan offers can be both time-consuming and daunting. Agents and credit brokers streamline this process by handling the legwork involved in identifying, comparing, and negotiating loan options. Their involvement can reduce the overall time to secure credit and often results in better loan terms, which can translate into significant cost savings over the life of a loan.

Credit intermediaries can also contribute to the integrity of the credit market by acting as a buffer between borrowers and lenders. They can help mitigate the risks associated with taking on new debt by advising clients on the potential pitfalls of various credit products and guiding them away from products that might be unsuitable or potentially harmful in the long term. This advisory role is particularly important in environments where predatory lending practices may be a concern.

However, the high-touch model also has limitations. It can be resource-intensive and may not scale efficiently in a digital age. The reliance on personal interactions can result in slower processes, higher operational costs and a limited reach, particularly among younger, tech-savvy demographics who prefer digital convenience.

On the other side of the spectrum is the "high tech" approach, based on online channels, which leverages digital interfaces, automation, and data analytics to transform financial services distribution. Key characteristics include:

- **Efficiency and Scalability:** Digital interfaces enable rapid processing of applications, seamless transactions and automated customer

support. This efficiency reduces turnaround times and operational costs while expanding access to a broader audience.
- **Data-Driven Insights:** High-tech solutions incorporate artificial intelligence and machine learning to analyse vast amounts of data, predict customer needs and personalise product offerings. This capability enhances risk management and helps in tailoring financial products to individual profiles.
- **Enhanced Accessibility:** Online platforms and mobile applications allow clients to access financial services anytime and anywhere, catering to a generation that values convenience and speed. Digital tools democratise financial services, reaching underserved markets and facilitating financial inclusion.

Despite its many advantages, the high-tech approach can sometimes fall short on personalisation. The digital interface may lack the nuanced understanding of human vulnerabilities, particularly when it comes to addressing complex financial challenges or emotional aspects of financial decision-making. Moreover, cybersecurity and data privacy remain persistent concerns that require robust safeguards.

The future of financial services distribution, then, likely lies in a hybrid model that integrates high touch with high tech. The debate between high touch and high tech in financial services distribution is not about choosing one over the other; rather, it is about harmonising these approaches to enhance customer experience and operational effectiveness. High touch provides the trust, empathy, and personalised service essential for complex financial decision-making and supporting vulnerable customers, while high tech delivers efficiency, scalability and data-driven insights that are indispensable in today's digital age. As financial institutions continue to innovate, striking the right balance between human interaction and technological advancement will be key to driving sustainable growth, fostering customer loyalty and ensuring robust, inclusive financial ecosystems.

These considerations are actually confirmed by a recent survey by OAM 2022[1] which showed that credit intermediaries and online channels are not seen by borrowers as hard alternatives but rather as complementary solutions. Mostly digitally literate consumers are actually advocating a strong and efficient combination of human touch and digital solutions

---

[1] AGENTI OAM E INNOVAZIONE FINANZIARIA. Analisi sui comportamenti dei consumatori nel 2022 https://www.organismo-am.it/documenti/csv/OAM-Survey_Agenti_Fintech_2022.pdf

that can reduce costs while, at the same time, ensuring the high level of service and personalisation that agents and credit brokers are credited for.

But there is also a new challenge and opportunity that credit intermediaries are facing. Bank branch closings have become a defining trend in the financial services landscape, driven by digital transformation, cost pressures and shifting consumer preferences. As traditional brick-and-mortar branches gradually recede, the role of agents and brokers is on the rise, reshaping how financial institutions distribute products and services.

Over the past decade, advancements in technology have fundamentally altered the way consumers interact with banks. Digital banking platforms, mobile applications and online financial services offer unparalleled convenience, enabling customers to perform routine transactions, access account information and even secure loans without stepping into a physical branch. In parallel, banks are under mounting pressure to reduce operational costs and increase efficiency. Maintaining a widespread network of branches, often in low-traffic areas, is increasingly seen as an expensive legacy cost. Consequently, many banks have opted to consolidate or close branches, redirecting resources toward digital channels and more profitable segments of their business.

As the physical footprint of banks diminishes, agents and brokers are stepping in to fill the distribution gap. They can provide critical touchpoints between consumers and financial institutions. Unlike traditional bank branches, agents and brokers typically operate with lower overhead costs while, at the same time, offering personalised, consultative services tailored to individual financial needs.

As agents work on behalf of banks, they serve as local representatives who can deliver a blend of high-touch, personalised service alongside digital tools. They help guide customers through more complex financial decisions, such as mortgage financing or credit solutions, which still require a human element for reassurance and clarity. Similarly, brokers work across multiple banks and lenders, offering clients a broader range of options and negotiating competitive terms on their behalf. Their extensive market knowledge and industry relationships enable them to provide insights that a purely digital interface might lack.

For consumers, the shift toward agents and brokers represents both opportunity and challenge. On one hand, the closure of branches may lead to concerns over reduced face-to-face service, particularly for individuals who value personal interaction or who may be less comfortable with digital interfaces. However, agents and brokers often provide a more flexible and accessible model, offering in-person consultations when needed while also harnessing technology to streamline processes and reduce costs.

For banks, leveraging agents and brokers can lead to a more efficient and scalable distribution model. This hybrid approach allows banks to maintain high levels of customer service without the significant cost burden associated with a large branch network. Moreover, by partnering with intermediaries who have specialised expertise, banks can more effectively target niche markets and complex product segments.

Regulatory changes, the impact of technology and evolving market conditions will further influence how banks structure their distribution channels. Institutions that successfully blend high-tech digital solutions with high-touch personal advisory services are poised to gain a competitive edge. In this evolving ecosystem, agents and brokers are not merely substitutes for physical branches but are integral components of a modern, agile distribution strategy.

On the other side, with banks reducing their branch networks, many consumers – particularly those in rural or underserved areas – face diminished access to in-person financial advice. Credit intermediaries can capitalise on this gap by offering personalised, accessible advisory services that were previously the exclusive domain of physical branches. Moreover, the reduced geographical constraints could enable brokers to tap into a broader, pan-European market, offering cross-border services where banks once dominated with localised branches. With fewer brick-and-mortar constraints, agents and brokers can operate leaner, reallocating resources to advanced digital tools and comprehensive market research, thereby enhancing operational efficiency and service quality.

Credit intermediaries also have an opportunity to address this gap by developing outreach programs and tailored services that cater to these underserved groups. By partnering with community organisations and leveraging mobile technology, they can enhance financial inclusion, thereby broadening their customer base while contributing to social equity.

However, to seize all the positive possibilities created by these evolutions, a common and stable regulation framework has to be established. By defining common standards across member states, harmonised regulation creates a more predictable and transparent legal environment that can enhance operational efficiency, foster consumer trust and enable cross-border expansion.

The first opportunity which a unified framework offers is the extension of credit intermediation services beyond national borders. Harmonised regulations should ensure that essential standards for licensing, consumer disclosure and professional conduct are made consistent across the EU. This uniformity would simplify compliance, reduce administrative overhead and allow agents and credit brokers to tap into larger markets with minimal legal barriers.

Looking at customers, harmonised regulation could greatly enhance consumer protection. With clear and consistent disclosure requirements and transparency rules, consumers would benefit from a higher level of protection regardless of their country of residence. For credit intermediaries, this means that the trust gap between intermediaries and consumers would be narrowed significantly. When consumers are confident that all credit intermediaries operate under the same high standards, they are more likely to seek out and use their services. This increased trust can lead to higher customer retention and attract new clients, ultimately contributing to a more robust and competitive market.

Uniform regulatory frameworks would facilitate the development of standardised licensing procedures and professional standards. Agents and credit brokers would certainly benefit from clearer guidelines regarding the qualifications and competencies required to operate, which in turn would help to elevate the overall professionalism within the industry. A level playing field would be established, reducing the incidence of substandard practices that can harm both consumers and the reputation of the industry. Enhanced standards also serve as a competitive advantage for firms that invest in higher levels of training and compliance, as they can market themselves as more reliable and consumer-friendly.

Harmonisation also reduces compliance costs and administrative burdens, which can have a direct positive impact on the efficiency of credit intermediation. With fewer bureaucratic hurdles and overlapping national regulations, agents and credit brokers could allocate more resources to service improvement and technological innovation. This operational efficiency would enable credit intermediaries to offer more competitive pricing and faster service delivery, also reducing the likelihood of regulatory arbitrage and fostering healthy market dynamics.

Finally, a harmonised regulatory framework would also pave the way for greater technological integration within the credit intermediation industry. Standardised rules create an environment in which innovative digital tools and platforms can be developed and deployed uniformly across the EU with an evident impact on economies of scale.

Open Access This chapter is licensed under the terms of the Creative Commons Attribution 4.0 International License (http://creativecommons.org/licenses/by/4.0/), which permits use, sharing, adaptation, distribution and reproduction in any medium or format, as long as you give appropriate credit to the original author(s) and the source, provide a link to the Creative Commons license and indicate if changes were made.

The images or other third party material in this chapter are included in the chapter's Creative Commons license, unless indicated otherwise in a credit line to the material. If material is not included in the chapter's Creative Commons license and your intended use is not permitted by statutory regulation or exceeds the permitted use, you will need to obtain permission directly from the copyright holder.

9783032059413